UNLEASH THE
P⬤WER
OF DIVERSITY

UNLEASH THE
P◯WER
OF DIVERSITY

Multi Cultural Competence
for Business Results

Dear Ian,
Hope you enjoy sharing this
Diversity Journey ('Foray') with
me, quich your formidable skills
and back ground!
Best Regards,
Debjani Mukherjea Biswas

DEBJANI MUKHERJEE BISWAS

authorHOUSE®

AuthorHouse™ LLC
1663 Liberty Drive
Bloomington, IN 47403
www.authorhouse.com
Phone: 1-800-839-8640

*Edited by * Barbara Weinberger * Niket Biswas * Ellen Linden*
*BACC Support by * Linda Smittle * Sandra Hoffman*
*Cover design by * Niket Biswas*

Published by AuthorHouse   07/25/2013

ISBN: 978-1-4817-6075-1 (sc)
ISBN: 978-1-4817-6074-4 (hc)
ISBN: 978-1-4817-6076-8 (e)

FIRST EDITION

Library of Congress Control Number: 2013910164

Acknowledgments

To my mother, Reba Mukherjee: you anchor my life with your deep and innate kindness, mental strength, and unconditional love. Your biggest gift is the unshaken belief that I can—and will—unleash the power that lies within us all.

To my family who are friends (some in spirit—Dadumoni, Bappi, Baba, and Kudy) and to friends who feel like family: the journey starts and ends with you.

To Marshall Goldsmith: your support and encouragement is a huge gift. "Thank you" seems inadequate.

To clients and session participants all over the world: this book is bolstered by the powerful learning and life experiences you trusted me with.

Finally, for every leader and individual who seeks to leverage diversity as a competitive advantage: this book is for you.

Advance praise from five continents and sixteen countries:

Austria: "Debjani Biswas is a brilliant and very inspirational woman. Her thorough knowledge and thinking in the intercultural field is what we need globally now more than ever."—*Cornelia Kalcher Tsuha, Founder of Global Success Coaching*

Australia: "I'm delighted to know that Debjani Biswas is sharing her expertise in *Unleash the Power of Diversity: Multi cultural Competence for Business Results.* Debjani's ideas are clear, groundbreaking, and practical. The learning from her ideas has continued to influence my interactions and ways of thinking in powerful ways. Once this book is available, I plan to devour more of Debjani's insights and frameworks for my own personal growth and for the development of my professional capacity to contribute to local and global communities characterized by respect and diversity."—*Andrea Dean*

Canada: "Debjani Biswas is an excellent communicator and someone who demonstrates a real commitment to supporting change. I appreciate Debjani's advocacy for diversity because now more than ever we need all hands on deck!"—*Alison Hendren, MCC, CEO of Coaching out of the Box ®*

Germany: "As an Indian female engineer who spent two decades working in corporate America, Debjani Biswas can relate to the topic of diversity with good reason. Considering her individual journey through life—her impressions, ideas, and the advice given in this book become tremendously authentic."—*Ladislaus von Daniels*

Ghana: "If you're searching for ways to increase your cross cultural effectiveness, immerse yourself in the Diversity Foray. With Debjani Biswas' inspired guidance and practical toolkit, you'll find yourself gazing into a mirror to see your cultural biases and examining options to improve everyday interactions. Using the tools provided, you can start adopting more effective behaviors and move towards becoming a diversity master."—*Linda Smittle, Peace Corps Volunteer*

India: "Debjani Biswas has, from a very young age, combined exceptional intelligence and diligence in equal measure. I wish her every success—in the certainty that she deserves every bit of it."—*Mondira Jha*

India: "Delighted that Debjani is synthesizing her vast experience into a book. Knowing her as I do, I am sure her book will be full of wisdom, yet eminently readable."—*Rupa Mahanty*

Japan: "I believe Debjani Biswas is walking and living diversity. I had several coincidence events—I would say 'synchronicity'—during the International Coach Federation global conference in 2012 in London with Debjani. I think synchronicity is one of the most important diversity concepts."—*Susumu Araki, CEO, Global Management Development Inc.*

Malaysia: "This book is a must read for everyone interested in learning about diversity from a new, out-of-the box perspective. Debjani is presenting a new model that addresses diversity using a unique 'engineering principles based' approach to cross cultural effectiveness. I am very happy to see how she has developed a set of very practical tools, using an original approach to leverage understanding between people from different cultures."—*Mario A. Bolanos*

Nigeria: "The first word that comes to mind when you meet Debjani is 'brilliant.' She has been successful in a male-dominated field and that requires much applause. Debjani is an inspiration to women in science fields and will always be successful in all she does."—*Ronke Okpa*

Norway: "With smart differentiation and use of colorful words and concepts, Debjani Biswas has captured and explained the essence of different diversity concepts. In an easy and fun way, she manages to take us on a journey to identify certain patterns in ourselves and others without judging. It makes me want to read the whole book!"—*Berit E. Ôhn, MCC, Accenture*

Sierra Leone: "Debjani Biswas' view of diversity as a strategy challenges us to leverage our rich, diverse, and multi cultural perspectives and insights and to make a difference in everyday interactions. This results in personal and professional development and growth, which, collectively, ultimately leads to organizational success. I am excited about the opportunities Debjani's counsel will unleash."—*Yinka Massally*

Singapore: "Knowing Debjani as I do, her book will be a huge success—not only for the thorough research she has done, but also for her analysis of this complex subject."—*Aditi Krishnakumar*

United Arab Emirates: "I am very privileged to have known Debjani Biswas. She is an inspirational role model. As her most recent accomplishment comes to light, I am very excited for her and wish her every success. I hope that her book contributes toward making our world a better place."—*Kshama Motha*

United Kingdom: "Debjani Biswas' Diversity Foray is a mind-shifting insight and practical tool kit I am now using with my day-to-day personal and corporate clients. Learn this original coaching tool and you will see direct benefit. What I particularly like is the combination of practical insights (as a former executive of a Fortune 50 company) and an engineering background, applied in original frameworks to solve emotional, business-related diversity issues."—*David Taylor, Vistage Group Chairman*

United States: "Debjani Biswas is a woman of amazing intelligence, managerial courage, and strategic vision. Her writing style is both professional and personal. I thoroughly enjoyed learning more about diversity while reading this book. It was as if I had my own diversity expert speaking to me in the same room."—*Barbara Weinberger*

United States: "Out of the box and into the fray: this challenging partnership of the mind and the written word strives to uplift our realization of human potential to levels that will help us—both singularly and collectively—to experience better days in the period ahead. I am proud to see Debjani Biswas blossom and grow."—*Shahrokh Nemazie*

Venezuela: "I believe in the power of diversity and consider Debjani Biswas to be a scholar when it comes to diversity. Through her personal and work life, she has been closely connected with the languages, culture, and work dynamics of the world. I wish Debjani much success in this book."—*Alberto Galue, PhD*

Preface

For years I have been asking myself these three questions:

* What would happen if one applied an engineering mindset of pattern recognition and data harvesting to the messy, complex, emotionally charged world of diversity and inclusion?
* What is the cost of cultural stereotyping in the workplace?
* Is there a simple framework and toolkit we can use to reduce these costs?

In short, how do we leverage multi cultural competence in an increasingly global workplace?

This book is the first step in answering these questions, based on three distinct building blocks.

First, the original frameworks:

- The Five Judgments (the process by which stereotyping occurs)
- A Diversity Foray (a practical toolkit for combating these limiting beliefs, with a series of dos and don'ts for greater cross cultural effectiveness)

Second, how does this play out in the real world? The practical "global toolkit" is designed to provide clear guidelines to navigate cross cultural diversity dilemmas at work. We explore unwritten rules of behavior, communication and appearance, and how they impact trust and reputation in the workplace.

Finally, this book serves as a handy reference guide and job aid for busy readers. This includes a digest of key concepts for critical segments, and tables on religious groups, countries and languages.

This book is a compilation of over two decades of corporate and individual observations from multiple cultures. It is founded on personal opinions, experiences, and anonymous qualitative responses from hundreds of workshop participants and clients from twenty-three countries.

As they say in Italian, divertitevi . . .

Unleash the Power of Diversity

"Life is a promise; fulfill it."
—Mother Teresa

CONTENTS

Section One
Laying the Foundation

Section Two
Introducing Original Frameworks

Section Three
Examining the Five Judgments

Section Four
Cultural Norms: a Practical Global Toolkit

Section Five
Conclusion

Appendix

Section One

Laying the Foundation

Analyzing how this book relates to your mission in life and assessing your readiness to start the diversity journey.

Chapter 1

Introduction

The journey of a thousand miles . . .

My fingers are trembling ever so slightly.

The date is October 17, 2012.

Today is the day I start the first book in this series: *Unleash the Power of Diversity: Multi Cultural Competence for Business Results."* Later on, we will examine practical features one routinely outlines in a book: the content of each section, new frameworks and conceptual challenges, business imperatives, and a call to action.

But for this moment, I want you to experience my heart beating a little bit faster.

To see the room around me, a Starbucks like so many others.

People typing, tutors with voices raised ever so slightly as they try to explain the difference between one type of differential equation or another.

The friendly man at the counter who says he doesn't remember my name or my order, but recognizes that "wonderful smile".

> I want you to feel it viscerally, in your stomach, because the work of diversity happens here. Not in our heads but in our guts, our hearts, and everywhere in between. That is why so much of what you read in this book will make you optimistic, angry, defensive, guilty, confused, or confident . . . emotional investment is a prerequisite for this book in order for it to have lasting personal and professional impact.

In a frenetic, stressful and deadline driven corporate environment, there is such a laser sharp focus on numbers and results that the human element is often forgotten.

Worse, we err on the side of compliance and conduct our annual diversity conference, appoint a diversity director or two, and feel competent at "diversity and inclusion."

The fact of the matter is that these measures, while positive, do not guarantee an engaged diverse workforce. And, on the premise that an engaged workforce is a more productive workforce, this book addresses the bottom line.

In order for true diversity learning to occur, however, the reader, regardless of whether she is the CEO of a multibillion-dollar multinational corporation or an individual contributor, must *be willing to read with both the head and the heart*. Therefore: *read the stories first* before going to the fact sheet that tells you how many Buddhists there are in the world or the map that highlights where the three billion Christians are located geographically. You will learn more that way. All adult learning and engagement theory validates that assumption.

So, shall we take a Diversity Foray together?

Author's note: I will define—and redefine—the word *foray* many times throughout this book. For now, it's a journey, an exploration, and also the framework that centers this book. The purpose of this framework is to offer a simple yet practical toolkit to make the complex, messy, often dangerous subject of diversity easier to explore.

Chapter 2

Mission

Setting our life compass

> *Why do we exist?*
>
> *If you don't know where you are going, you can read a thousand books with topics and techniques to help you improve your life, and it will not make much of a difference in the end.*
>
> *I don't mean to talk you out of reading this book on diversity, but truthful I must be!*
>
> *So before we start talking about diversity, culture, and all the other aspects that make us different, let's center ourselves.*

What is your mission in life?

Do you have five or six words that serve as your "north star" and guide your life?

A wise man I met recently—a master in meditation and immensely learned—said that his is *Peace on earth*. An attendee at a recent global conference showed me his card; it said simply *Clarity wins*.

My north star is *Learning, teaching, helping with graceful flawed authenticity.*

Each of those words represents something very critical.

- If it moves others forward, sharing what I have learned matters to me; this mutual process also enables *continuous learning* from others—thus, *learning, teaching, helping*.

- *Graceful* is about dealing with life's challenges with equanimity.

- *Flawed* is because our human failings, along with our strengths, make us who we are. We must therefore accept the negative traits that inevitably accompany our strengths.

- *Authenticity* is because I have worn masks, relentlessly, for many years of my life, particularly after moving from an Asian to a North American work environment. Many of the norms I grew up with seemed unacceptable compared to the new norms. *We all wear masks; I just want mine to be transparent and rarely used.*

Setting the context

Having a mission statement ensures that one has an internal compass for one's actions. It is what gives us direction through life. Answering the question—*Where does this diversity book fit in with your mission?*—will create a frame of reference as you read. Having more than one reason to read the book would be a bonus. *In order to answer this question, you must first have a mission.*

If you feel that you already have a clear, compelling mission, please move to page **12** and skip the *create a mission* activity on the next page.

First examine your mission and then see if the exploration of diversity is part of your direction in life. For example, the person whose mission is *Clarity first* may add to this clarity by learning about different peoples. ***Peace on Earth*** as a mission is aided by understanding people from other cultures.

> ➢ If you already have a strong mission, skip page **11** and directly fill out your mission on page **12** (Mission Statement). If not, complete your mission on page **11** first (or at least develop a draft mission) and continue.

Quotes to inspire your thinking *(these are not mission statements, just catalytic ideas)*:

➢ "We need to give each other the space to grow, to be ourselves, to exercise our diversity. We need to give each other space so that we may both give and receive such beautiful things as ideas, openness, dignity, joy, healing, and inclusion."—Max de Pree

➢ "Be daring, be different, be impractical, be anything that will assert integrity of purpose and imaginative vision against the play-it-safers, the creatures of the commonplace, the slaves of the ordinary."—Cecil Beaton

➢ "We find comfort among those who agree with us, growth among those who don't."—Frank Clark

➢ "Simplicity is the ultimate sophistication."—Leonardo Da Vinci

➢ "Be who you are and say what you feel because those who mind don't matter and those who matter don't mind."—Dr. Seuss

➢ "I will not let anyone walk through my mind with their dirty feet."—Mahatma Gandhi

➢ "No one can make you feel inferior without your consent."—Eleanor Roosevelt

➢ "If we cannot now end our differences, at least we can help make the world safe for diversity."—John F Kennedy

➤ "We inhabit a universe that is characterized by diversity."—Desmond Tutu

➤ "To speak gratitude is courteous and pleasant, to enact gratitude is generous and noble, but to live gratitude is to touch Heaven."—Johannes A. Gaertner

➤ "We all should know that diversity makes for a rich tapestry, and we must understand that all the threads of the tapestry are equal in value no matter what their color."—Maya Angelou

Developing a Mission Statement:

If you don't already have a mission and would like to develop one, follow the steps listed below.

a. What is my mission? Write important words and phrases here.

_____
_____
_____

Select less than ten words that will guide you in the future.

_____
_____

Sample Mission Statements:

Learning, teaching, helping with graceful flawed authenticity.

Peace on earth.

b. Your mission (it may be necessary to revisit this over time).

_____

_____

_____

- Does this mission statement serve as your compass?
  - Can you test future actions based on it?
  - Is learning about diversity congruent with your mission? (The word diversity doesn't have to be in your mission statement, just aligned with your direction.)
- If you answered *yes*, you are ready to start the journey/Diversity Foray with us.

Author's note: There are several great techniques and ways to complete one's Mission Statement. Some of them involve two-day retreats in Sonoma or the Loire Valley with yoga and massages and spiritual music. All of these techniques for arriving at a mission can be highly effective; I have personally used some of these options to refine my mission. In the absence of a formal visioning experience, drafting a mission statement is a valuable first step in this journey.

My reasons for reading this book are:

_____

_____

_____

_____

Select as many of the choices below that apply, and add your own reasons.

For example:

- I want to increase the morale of my diverse workforce.
- Diversity and inclusion are very important to me professionally and personally.
- I live in a country where I look and feel different. It would help me to understand how to integrate into the mainstream without losing my identity.
- I want to know more about cultures of the world in order to increase my interpersonal effectiveness.
- I manage a cross cultural team in this country.
- I conduct business regularly with people from other geographic locations.
- I will soon be working in/with _____ country.
- My son-in-law/best friend/boss (insert word here) is from another culture and I really want to improve my understanding of—and relationship with—him or her.

Chapter 3

Culture Defined

> *Culture is the way you behave*
> *when you think no one's*
> *looking . . .*

What is 'Culture'?

Culture definitions differ in the context of business and anthropological literature. Both disciplines, however, reference culture as being the *norms, values, and beliefs of a group of people,* typically tied together by a common ethnicity, race, or religion. My definition of culture, based on observations and experience, is that *culture is the way you behave when you think no one's looking.*

We could speak about a culture based on country, general region, or religion such as the "Muslim culture" (the context of which would be religion: as in the role of Islamic women in society), the "Middle East" (here referring to a region), or "Saudi Arabia" (a country within the Middle East), which happens to be predominantly Muslim (following the religion of Islam).

It is critical to understand which culture we are referencing, because not all countries within the Middle Eastern Islamic culture have the same norms with respect to women's rights, in the example referenced. A woman from Iran may have both Islamic as well as Persian beliefs, which result in a different set of role expectations.

Stereotypes are defined as a set of beliefs, both positive and negative, about a group.

For example, a popularly held belief is that a male from China will be good at math, and—by extension—also book smart and intelligent. That is a positive stereotype.

Stereotyping often occurs in clusters; therefore, this same man may also be associated with negative stereotypes such as "introverted, no sense of humor, etc."

I want to make sure that I am very clear here. *This is not my opinion of people from China or Iran*; am just defining culture and stereotypes. Without belaboring the point, please understand that these examples are used merely to illustrate the concepts.

There is a tendency toward defensiveness that takes away from learning when we approach the subject of stereotyping.

Imagine you have an ugly little baby. You may personally be a bit disappointed at its little red face with a huge nose; as parents may even joke with your spouse about it. How would you feel, however, if someone *else* calls your baby ugly? Cultural diversity work often feels (in the gut and heart) like someone is *calling your baby ugly.*

Recognize it. This is all part of the journey of self-discovery.

Beliefs are "unconscious DVDs" (or tapes, depending on one's age!) that keep playing in the mind, like soft music.

Our norms and beliefs lie at the core of our culture. These beliefs can be positive or negative, limiting or liberating.

In addition to culture, there are other factors. Life experiences, socioeconomic background, and gender messaging also have a strong impact on belief systems. We act out our beliefs on a daily basis.

For example, when a mother tells her third grade son: "Wait till your dad gets home for help with your math homework," she is exhibiting her belief that third grade math is too difficult for her. Over time, her son will probably also develop this belief. His belief will be that women are unlikely to succeed in STEM (Science, Technology, Engineering and Math) careers, but he may be unable to pinpoint the source of this unconscious typecasting. Limiting belief systems leads to stereotyping, which translates from the home to the workplace. Now let's bring it back to the business implications.

Author's note: I find it very distracting to read *his/her* and *he/she* in books. Therefore, for easier readability, I reference *her personal brand* and *his hidden self* in the book to vary pronoun gender. Upon first editing the manuscript, it was surprising to note that I had cited significantly more *he* examples than *she*. Though I took care of the anomaly, it was eye-opening to uncover this personal hidden bias.

Why do we care about cultural stereotyping in the workplace?

- The most critical reason is that **we make poor selection, recruitment, promotion, and layoff** decisions, which, over time, result in **significant productivity losses and opportunity costs.**

- When negative stereotyping occurs, **a lot of energy is wasted** in defusing and handling the situation.
- The person **being stereotyped typically shuts down,** either literally in terms of work output, or verbally.
- The person doing the stereotyping often feels poorly treated as well and **defensively forms a clique.** This then quickly turns into an us versus them situation.
- To summarize: **stereotyping leads to ineffective, subjective, and costly decisions;** additionally, **productive energy has to be diverted from the business task** at hand in order to defuse destructive interpersonal conflicts.

Chapter 4

Self-Assessment

What is my brand? What are my biases, stereotypes and limiting beliefs?

On the following two pages, fill out an honest self-assessment of your personal brand, presence, and cultural biases. Please note this will be very difficult to fill out, particularly the part about your hidden biases.

Author's note: For legal reasons it is inadvisable to leave self-assessments (particularly stereotypes, etc.) lying around, especially in a work environment as there are obvious legal repercussions related to this topic area. Please exercise common sense and good judgment in all aspects of reading and using this book.

The purpose of this exercise is to increase your self-awareness. This in turn, can translate to better business results through greater cross cultural effectiveness. Please be honest; only you will determine who views your responses.

Part One: Personality and Brand

What is my personal brand and presence?

- I am more like a * Hammer * Brush (circle one choice only).
  - I know this because _____.
  - Most people from my culture are * Hammers * Brushes
    - Hammers are hard-hitting, blunt, honest, results-oriented and deadline-driven people
      - Under stress, hammers hit the nail so hard the wall cracks.
    - Brushes are pleasant, likeable, hate to hurt people's feelings
      - Under stress, brushes smooth so much paint on the damaged wall that it cracks.
    - Most people are a combination, obviously. If you are not sure which one you are more like, ask someone who knows you well. Be prepared for their honest answer!

- I'm too _____ .
  - I know this because _____ .
  - Most people from my culture are * similar * different in this aspect.

- I'm not _____ enough.
  - I know this because _____ .
  - Most people from my culture are * similar * different in this aspect.

- An engaging characteristic of mine is _____
  _____ .
  - I know this because _____ .
  - Most people from my culture are * similar * different in this aspect.

Part Two: Biases and Beliefs

What are my stereotypes and biases?

- I would be very uncomfortable if my _____ (child / sibling/relative) married a _____ (ethnic descriptor).
    - This is because _____.

- I really like people from _____ (location).
    - This is because _____.

- I feel uncomfortable around people who look _____ _____ (cultural characteristic).
    - This is because _____.

- If my car broke down at night in _____, I would be really nervous.
    - This is because _____.

- I connect most with people who are _____ _____ (cultural descriptor).
    - This is because _____.

- I am afraid of people from _____ (this religion).
    - This is because _____.

- Insert your own biases here. (They could have been learned in childhood or developed through personal experiences as an adult.) _____ _____ _____ _____

Additional notes based on the exercise:

_____

If you are uncomfortable documenting your responses, mentally answer the questions and process the learning internally.

Chapter 5

Emotional Intelligence

Before we come to the original diversity frameworks and concepts introduced in this book, let us add a little background. *Diversity exploration begins with basic emotional intelligence.* There are three thought leaders who have helped build the concept of emotional intelligence that resonate most with me. They are Daniel Goleman, Howard Gardner, and David Wechsler. The essential focus, for our purpose, is the difference between emotional and academic "intelligence."

Emotional intelligence (EI) focuses on our self-awareness and self-management, and our ability to empathize, manage relationships, be socially savvy, and motivate others.

For decades, there has been a heated debate about the importance of EQ (Emotional Quotient) versus IQ (Intelligence Quotient). Anecdotal observations suggest that *people are selected for technical skills* but succeed, or fail, based on emotional savvy. In other words people are often hired into positions based on their IQ, education, college, and technical skills. Once in organizations, *their success (whether they are fired, promoted, or obtain a followership) is based on intrapersonal and interpersonal skills, versus technical abilities.*

Emotional intelligence is an important concept in diversity work for two reasons.

First of all, because *cultural diversity often uncovers deep seated prejudices, biases and stereotypes.* These are typically judgmental thoughts of *right versus wrong.* Therefore, a person who is low in emotional intelligence—particularly self-awareness, empathy, recognition of personal cues, and "hot buttons"—will struggle in diversity exploration. This will have a multiplier effect, as a lack of self-awareness will translate into a corresponding inability to self manage.

The second reason is that the ability to remain authentic while "fitting into a new environment" requires social awareness, another key component of emotional intelligence.

How emotional intelligence helps us defend against diversity onslaughts:

In 1990, we moved from Lafayette, Indiana to Dallas, Texas. In my undergraduate engineering days, interviewing people on TV and conducting basic game shows (in English, of course) had earned me a side income. So I called a local TV station to inquire about part-time opportunities.

The woman on the line asked "Is this for you?" When I replied that *yes, this was for me*, she responded *"Don't bother to turn in an application; there is no place in US TV for someone who sounds like you."* In the last twenty-two years, I have developed significantly higher emotional intelligence, particularly in self-management. But, at that moment, upon hearing those words, it is hard to describe the feelings that went through my mind and body. I literally had a sick feeling in my stomach—a combination of anger, disbelief, shame, and embarrassment. What makes this example noteworthy is the context around the situation.

I was a successful engineer and MBA who had worked in a prestigious organization (Tata Administrative Services) and I was fortunate enough to have a family that gave me unconditional love and support. *For decades, there had been visible rewards attached to my speaking in English*: television and radio experiences, over a hundred prizes for debate, elocution, and drama, as well as the experience of being the Master of Ceremonies at large events.

> And yet, *this one comment—made by a nameless, faceless stranger—made me experience shame and embarrassment* about the way I spoke. It wasn't because of a physical change due to a speech impediment or natural causes. I now had an undesirable *foreign* accent relative to the mainstream population, purely as a result of having changed locations.

Over the years, as my emotional intelligence developed, there were situations where it was possible to leverage the strong emotions associated with that comment to push myself further.

Did this event harness more energy toward positive actions, fueled by emotional power? Or did it cause setbacks because of a newfound diffidence or self-consciousness?

The answer remains unclear, but these are the questions that must be asked as we receive diversity wounds and sometimes bleed or run away; sometimes stand firm and try to make the other bleed. The discerning reader will realize that most of the options listed are not productive, which is the point of this example.

This book is designed to provide you with tools so that, when someone tells you, a diverse person, that you can "never succeed because you are different," you can be diversity adept, and do two things:

➢ Harness your emotional intelligence to recognize your emotions at that moment.
➢ Manage your response to match the *presence* or *brand* you would like to project.

> React objectively when you feel attacked, allowing you an element of power and truly increasing your impact. Even if it's as simple as the recognition: "I am close to lashing out right now. This would benefit the attacker and hurt my brand at work. The best option is to walk away and re-engage when I can speak coherently and calmly."

If you can inject a pinch of humor (regarding the offending party, preferably), your brain stops acting like a Neanderthal; your breathing calms down and normalcy returns.

If you are the leader or mentor of someone in this situation, this book is designed to help you coach the individual concerned, and also—on a systematic and systemic basis—reduce the occurrence of such situations.

In order to change an unpleasant reality associated with cultural diversity, one must have a realistic view of the relationships, both interpersonal and societal, in which one functions. One should also have a realistic awareness of one's relative powers and abilities to influence others and affect large scale change. Emotional intelligence is, therefore, a prerequisite for significant and systematic progress to occur.

To summarize, key emotional intelligence concepts include:

Self-Awareness: Accuracy of gauging one's emotions, and how we come across to others

Self-Management: Ability to control one's emotions, patience, anger, and optimism

Social Awareness: Organizational awareness of climate, group dynamics, and empathy

Relationship Management: Inspiring others, managing conflict, change, and collaborating

Which aspects will help us most in our diversity foray?

While understanding that all parts of the EI model are important, perhaps the most critical and basic step involves increasing our self-awareness.

I typically combine high-level concepts of Emotional Intelligence with a deep dive into self-awareness using the well-known *Johari Window*.

Chapter 6

Johari Window

What is the *Johari Window*?

- It sounds exotic, but the name came from a *Joe* and a *Harry* putting their names together to define a truly simple, yet powerful, self-awareness tool.
- Devised by Joseph (Joe) Luft and Harry Ingham in 1955, the Johari Window has been used as a Disclosure or Feedback model of self-awareness, worldwide, for half a century. It is also referred to by some as an *information-processing tool*.
- There are multiple Johari Window explanations available. While some use 'Rooms' instead of 'Quadrants' or have Quadrants in different locations, the key learning remains the same. Essentially, that it is important to be aware of what we, and others, know or do not know, about ourselves/us.
- I apply this in the context of diversity because cultural blind spots and lack of awareness hinder our progress. This becomes less of a barrier when we open the Johari window panes.

Known Self	Hidden Self
Things *we know* about ourselves that *others also know* about us	Things *we know* about ourselves that *others do not know* about us
Blind Self	Unknown Self
Things *others know* about us that *we do not know* about ourselves	Things *others do not know* about us that *we also do not know* about ourselves

The x (horizontal) axis refers to *others' knowledge of us*, which is high in quadrants 1 and 3.

The y (vertical) axis refers to *our knowledge of ourselves*, which is high in quadrants 1 and 2.

- *Quadrant 1 Known Self*: We know this about ourselves and others know this about us. It's the open window—transparent. For example, when a boy is six years old, he proudly shares his age with the world around him. He says, "I am six and a quarter," and this is a fact that is known to him and all those around him who are willing to listen.
- *Quadrant 2 Hidden Self:* Here are things that people start hiding from others, even though they know them to be true. An attractive, well-preserved man may start building stories of his past and carefully imply things to make himself younger than he is . . . particularly when meeting an attractive young woman at a bar. He starts hiding things or not responding to questions about when

he finished college, or how long he's been working—in order to keep his "hidden self" hidden.

- *Quadrant 3 Blind Self:* Continuing with age-related examples for this quadrant, this is the man who dyes his hair jet black at seventy-five. He believes that this makes him look young and people don't have the heart to tell him the truth. Others know that the contrast—between his black hair and his wrinkled face, rheumy eyes, thinning hair, and bare spots of protruding scalp—is a cruel joke . . . and actually makes him look older. But the "blind self" makes the man incapable of seeing this when he looks in the mirror.

- *Quadrant 4 Unknown Self.* This is the quadrant that shows us things about ourselves that neither we, nor others, could have known ahead of time. It is often described as "grace under pressure" when our unknown self responds positively or falls to pieces when we crumble under pressure. In 2011, seven-year-old Drew Champagnie from New York made a 911 call that saved his mother's life. His mother was having a seizure, but Drew maintained his composure and gave emergency respondents his address and enough information for them to reach them in a timely manner. In fact, Drew was awarded "junior EMT" status at a special ceremony to acknowledge his heroic actions. *Neither Drew, nor his mother, could have known this fact about him ahead of time; it was part of Drew's "unknown self."* After the event occurred, though, now his grace under pressure and ability to think quickly in an emergency moved from quadrant 4 to quadrant 1. This applies in both positive and negative examples; someone who we predict will be tough under pressure may, in fact, fall to pieces in a crisis. As soon as the event occurs, once again, this weakness moves from being unknown (quadrant 4) to hidden (quadrant 2).

This brings up an interesting point about the Johari Window. There are things that we consciously choose to move up and down quadrants, based on our perception of the risk of openness and consequences.

So, which panes will help us most in diversity effectiveness?

While all the panes can be informative, most of the diversity work we do in cross cultural effectiveness relates to quadrants 2 (hidden self) and 3 (blind self).

What are we hiding about ourselves? When a person comes from a different culture into a mainstream situation in which he is the only representative of his group, he often feels forced to hide facts about his culture in order to gain acceptance. It feels like the weight of the world—or at least his country or religion—is on his shoulders.

What might a person from a minority group hide?

- How often he bathes or shampoos
- Her religion, its tenets, and her deeply held beliefs
- What meats his culture eats
- How her marriage came about
- How many years he lived at home with his parents
- How full of potholes the roads are in her native country
- Whether policemen take bribes or beat prisoners
- How corrupt politicians are "back home"
- Whether his parents will live with him when they grow old
- How many children she shared a room with in her childhood
- How many days he wore/wears the same clothes to save on cleaning costs
- How many people squeezed into one car/scooter/cycle/bus

- That it makes her sick to her stomach to see people on TV playing with chocolate pudding as food is sacred and not to be disrespected

Can you begin to believe what this takes out of a man, day after day, when he has to skate on thin ice? Never knowing when a question may come to take him off guard? He worries that letting his guard down will (in his mind, at least) result in being seen as even *more* of an outsider than he already is. The next time he is having a cup of coffee at his office cafeteria, someone may come up to him and say, "You know, I saw on the TV/internet/blog that people in your country . . ."

- slit the neck of cows and drink their blood
- worship rats
- eat dogs

Bam, just like that.

You never know when or where an unsettling event will occur.

This is a low danger by itself, but over time it makes the person more and more cautious and less willing to be real about the culture he came from. Many people from different cultures develop a few stock responses by way of repartee. Depending on their style and personality, some rebuttals are, in fact, counter attacks. Offense is used as a form of defense, for instance, such as:

- "Well, *I* heard on the news that persons in this country steal/are homeless/marry more than once/have ten children/are illiterate/are corrupt."

Another way people deal with this is to appear to give in, on the surface. This complete agreement, or absence of overt resistance, may actually be an extreme case of bringing the hidden self to play.

For the reader who believes that this is a relatively insignificant dynamic, let me caution you. These real life examples from around the world often significantly—and emotionally—impacted the people experiencing them.

Quadrant 3, the Blind Self, is equally important in diversity exploration.

- People from different cultures and ethnic backgrounds make judgments on others based on their frames of reference.
- The person from a diverse culture often truly does not understand her personal *brand* or image.
- Having a trusted friend, advisor, or mentor who gives caring feedback can effectively increase awareness of one's blind spots.
- Some examples would be for the advisor or mentor to suggest that the person's way of dressing is giving a poor first impression in a job interview.
- Another blind spot relates to hygiene. For example, people from some Western countries (particularly the United States) are considered obsessive about hygiene and cleanliness. People in Asian and European countries crack jokes (behind their backs) about things like Americans going to third world countries and bathing their children in bottled mineral water (in case some dirty tap water falls into the baby's mouth).

For Diversity work, we typically explore four key aspects of Diversity:

- Culture
- Gender
- Generation
- Style

Therefore, while this book focuses on a critical aspect of what makes us different at the workplace, in isolation it is not enough.

In diversity work, in order to come up with statistically valid findings, *we need to allow for more than one aspect of diversity*. This book's approach is qualitative and based on examples. Since I have had access to hundreds of cross cultural data points over the last twenty years, there may be some fuzzy patterns of evidence (if one can classify grouped anecdotal data as evidence) that support some of these theories. But keep in mind, until an enterprising PhD student takes one of these hypotheses and runs a rigorous statistical regression and data analysis, we will not have empirical proof.

While we are on that train of thought, here's another hypothesis.

I speculate that the variance (R^2) of a person's behavior, explained by different diversity aspects (culture, gender, generation and style) is directly proportionate to the uniqueness of that aspect, in that situation. This is strikingly evident, according to my hypothesis, if that person is a "sole representative" of that diversity factor. The term I have coined to explain this phenomenon is *Distinguishing Markers*, which will be explained in Section Two as part of the new framework, "The Five Judgments."

To elaborate, I am an *Asian female baby boomer* with a certain *behavioral style; ENTJ* (in Myers Briggs or MBTI terminology): mild extravert, strategic thinker, logic based decision-maker, organized list maker.

When in India (or other parts of Asia), my culture-based behaviors will be similar to the mainstream population. Therefore, another diversity factor (being the only female engineer in a group of male engineers, for example) will define people's perception of my being different, not my being Asian.

However, at an organizational development conference in Australia, where the majority of the participants is female, and in my age group, my "style" may be what distinguishes me from others.

Why is this concept important? We speculate about what makes a person different. *We assume that someone's culture explains every aspect of her behavior.* That is not accurate. A colleague who recently e-mailed me is entering into a business situation with someone from India. He said, "This person's name is Shirish Godbole (name changed for confidentiality). Can you tell me something about him that will help in my business dealings?"

Imagine someone coming up to you and asking, "I am going to meet a person called John Smith. Based on his name, can you tell me something about him?"

Hard to do, perhaps?

The reason this question was somewhat reasonable is that there are fewer Shirish Godboles in the United States than

John Smiths. So I could guess the specific region he came from and a couple of other things about him.

Beware of cultural diversity charlatans or zealots.

When you have a hammer in your hand, somehow everything starts to look like a nail. So it is with cultural diversity work. Yes, culture *can* explain a lot of our behavioral differences in the workplace. However, other critical diversity factors—such as gender, generation, or style—must also be taken into account. Otherwise, we may be irresponsibly inaccurate in our speculations.

To summarize, the first section contains general concepts that apply to other diversity aspects: *Culture *Style *Gender *Generation. Furthermore, many of the original frameworks and tools presented in the book may be applied to solve broader leadership issues.

Key Learning from Section One: Laying the Foundation

- Everything starts with a mission in life—one's purpose or reason for being.
- Emotional Intelligence, particularly self-awareness and self-management, is critical in diversity work.
- Knowing one's personal brand or presence is critical.
- Culture is the set of values, norms, customs, rituals, and traditions held in common by a group of people. The author's definition of culture is: *the way we behave when no one is looking.*
- Culture is used in this book to describe a country, religion, or geographical region.
- To be cross culturally effective, you must assess yourself honestly and openly; it takes courage to look closely at one's own prejudices, stereotypes, and biases.
- Stereotypes are beliefs about a group of people, both positive and negative.
- *Limiting beliefs* are internal boundaries or gateways that stop people from reaching their full potential.
- In an era of information overload, stereotypes are used as a heuristic (rule) to break information down into manageable chunks.
- The Johari Window is a self-discovery tool looking at what we—and others—know about us. The four quadrants of the Johari Window are: Known, Hidden, Blind, and Unknown Self.
- As you start to explore these areas, be aware of masks people wear when they are perceived as being different.
- Diversity work resides mainly in the gut and the heart, not the head.
- Well meaning, tactless questions can be seen as attacks on the diverse person's culture.

- People who live outside their birthplace can see cultural insults where they do not exist.
- Reacting objectively under duress can exponentially increase your power and impact.
- A careless comment can devastate an otherwise successful and well-balanced person.
- After taking the self-assessment of your own presence and brand, decide if you want to adjust your power and impact while remaining authentic.

Section Two

Introducing Original Frameworks

This section focuses on the two concepts that
are the basis of this book.

The Five Judgments: analyzing the cost of
stereotyping in the workplace

A Diversity Foray: outlining the *Do's* and *Don'ts* of
cross cultural effectiveness

'It ain't what you don't know that gets you in trouble:
It's what you know for sure that just ain't so."
—*Mark Twain*

Chapter 7

The Five Judgments: the cost of stereotyping in the workplace

I started this book with a premise: *as leaders, we have an obligation to ensure world-class business practices.* This will lead to higher productivity and a more engaged workforce. Leveraging diversity wisely gets us to a *more stable, motivated workforce.* That was the *why* or the purpose of this book.

In this section, I add the *how*: the tools that will *help get us to that desired outcome.*

The Five Judgments is an original framework that relates to the cost of stereotyping in the workplace.

The objective of this section is to logically and methodically outline the sequence and impact of five critical judgments that are made about a person.

The application of the Five Judgments is far-reaching. It is relevant in interviewing, selection, job allocation, performance review, high performance development, and a host of other workplace situations.

What are the Five Judgments?

In the course of workplace interactions, there are powerful behavioral forces at play that most people are completely oblivious to. The Five Judgments framework is designed to analyze and categorize these forces.

In a nutshell, my hypothesis is that five powerful conclusions are reached, consciously and unconsciously, about people at work, some of which are directly linked to cultural stereotyping.

The outcome of these judgments is to label a person on a positive or negative continuum on certain characteristics. This label follows that individual throughout his career and has significant ramifications on his ultimate success in the workplace.

The five judgments are based upon:

- Reputational Currency (buzz)
- Physical Impact (appeal)
- Auditory Cues (sound)
- Distinguishing Markers (differentiators)
- Work Product (output)

A separate chapter is devoted to each of these elements in the next section, so it is enough to grasp the basic premise during the introductory phase.

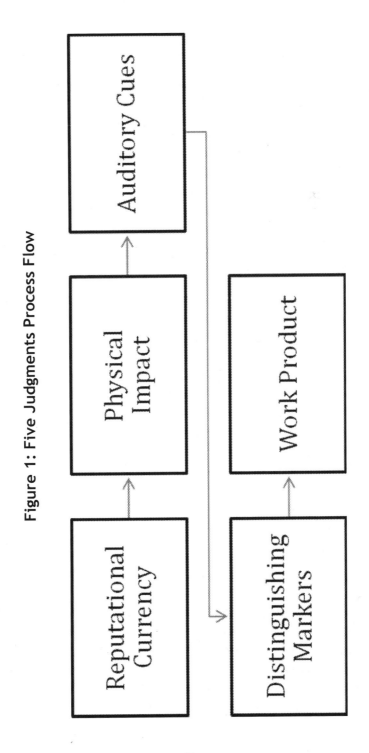

Figure 1: Five Judgments Process Flow

The Five Judgments overview:

Reputational Currency: Long before you personally interact with a person at the office or workplace, she has preconceived notions of you. This could be based on your individual brand, word of mouth, or social media. If there is no data about you as a person, she will make *the first judgment* of you based on cultural stereotyping and unconscious biases.

Physical Impact: As soon as you interact with this person, she forms *the second judgment* of you based on two key components of physical impact: your visual appeal and your freshness quotient. Visual appeal relates to your innate physical appeal, as well as attire and accessories. This includes your apparent age range, perceived attractiveness, trendiness, and executive presence. Critical to cultural judgments, your freshness quotient starts with how you smell. *Body odor is the kiss of death, an unconscious rejection at first whiff.* More unconscious factors include (in the absence of body odor) the subtle messaging of your fragrance. Baby powder, faint but expensive cologne, or perfume—all of these signal a certain message.

Auditory Cues: *The third judgment* is formed based on pitch and tone of voice, giggles versus laughter, as well as the volume, speed, and number of words used. *The cultural overlay to this judgment manifests itself first in the accent, and next in the choice of vocabulary.* Unconsciously held beliefs cause us to judge the same thing differently depending on our frame of reference; for example, *using long words may be viewed negatively as being old-fashioned.* On the other hand, *an extensive vocabulary may be viewed positively* in another culture as a sign of intellectual ability.

Distinguishing Markers: What is unique or different about you? *This fourth judgment* is particularly critical in cross-cultural effectiveness exploration. If the only thing you remember about a person is that he has a long beard and a turban, or that she is wearing a veil that covers her face, that is defined as a *distinguishing marker—for that individual, in that situation, with that person. A distinguishing marker in one culture may not be categorized as such in another.* This applies, in particular, to group characteristics such as religion.

Work Product: *The fifth judgment* relates to our output: its quality and how original it is as well as how much we can produce in a given amount of time. In an interview situation, output is measured by incomplete data such as timeliness, samples, and PowerPoint presentation quality. The most interesting learning here is that, typically, *four judgments occur before one even starts to examine a person's output.*

These judgments result in an overall "score" and placement of that individual, which can have a powerful effect on their success or failure at work. *This critical first impression* is supplemented over time by *perceived future behavior and performance.* First impressions are often more important than actual results.

Sum of Five Judgments:	*The Orchid Effect*
A quick mental synthesis of all behavioral factors, data, and sensory inputs	An overall impression, ranking, or placement is made about this person and stored in the subconscious. This is powerful and often automatic. This label affects future hiring, promotion, and attrition—decisions that could cost the organization millions.

This is called the Orchid Effect because the orchid has a brand for being unusual or different. The question is, does being different make people assume, after the five judgments, that you are rare and valuable like an orchid? *Or are your differences working against you?*

Elements of the Five Judgments

Judgment	Factors of Influence
Buzz	People's comments about you, previous perceptions about people "like you" (in the viewer's mind)—based on education, cultural interactions, past experiences
Appearance	Intrinsic physical characteristics, age range, and appeal
	External additions: clothes, shoes, and accessories
	Body odor, trace spices, pleasant fragrances (uniquely critical in cross cultural effectiveness work)
Sound	Tone and pitch of voice
	Gravitas or silliness in demeanor
	Fluency, coherence, vocabulary, and language choice
Differentiators	What is one thing that stands out about you?
	What do people remember about you when you leave?
	Are you outside the normal or expected range for anything? (for example, either too short, thin, ethnically dressed, talkative, nervous, or qualified)
Output	Perception of quality (packaging, delivery, and content)
	Timeliness for deadlines and meetings

We will only achieve real breakthroughs in the workplace if we inoculate ourselves against stereotyping and limiting beliefs. Once the five judgments' concepts and pathology are clear, how you apply them in day-to-day business settings will be up to you.

If being different is working for you, leverage the differences.

If being different is working against you, use the five factors to analyze and adjust your impact, while remaining authentic.

The primary purpose is to make the unconscious conscious, particularly when it comes to uncovering brand and personal presence.

On the flip side, it's recognizing how we automatically judge entire groups of people or disregard potential organizational stars, based on long-held limiting beliefs. This is particularly important when navigating cultural diversity, as the norms change from under us when we move locations, often without our realizing it. The phenomenon outlined has to do with how one is judged (when different from the local population) based on five specific areas.

Applications of the five judgments at work:

Our credentials are usually based on word-of-mouth, reputation and—in the current milieu—social media presence. Tech-savvy millennials in particular are changing the spelling of their names (taking out vowels or using creative alternatives) in order to nullify the potential damage of this judgment.

In the absence of such data, people make prejudgments based on which group they think you belong to—that is, what they think you represent, or are affiliated with. How does this manifest itself?

Lesley Stahl featured a segment on TV's reputed *60 Minutes* focusing on the Indian Institute of Technology (IIT) engineering school system. The exact quote was: *"Put Harvard, MIT, and Princeton together, and you begin to get an idea of the status of IIT in India. IIT is dedicated to producing world-class chemical, electrical, and computer engineers with a curriculum that may be the most rigorous in the world."* As soon as this program aired, people who connected the dots (that I graduated from IIT with a degree in chemical engineering) assumed a high degree of intelligence, coupled with strong, practical technical skills even though *I had never worked in the United States as an engineer.*

These are units of what I call "reputational currency" which precede meeting a person from a different population.

At the moment of initial contact, the person makes three more judgments, based on how you *look, smell, sound, and behave, particularly when something is different about you.* These three judgments occur almost simultaneously. Sensory inputs (such as whether you giggle or nod, interrupt, and have good eye contact) are a core part of these judgments as well.

Finally, the tangible product or deliverable, your output, enters the overall equation. This includes more objective activities (such as patterns of punctuality, typos on emails, quality, and relevance of content).

Much of diversity coaching can be applied to general business performance. Therefore, awareness and self-management of the five judgments has *the added bonus of assisting anyone at the workplace*, even the mainstream population. In other words, regardless of whether you are culturally diverse or not, *understanding the five judgments can positively impact your professional and personal brand.*

To summarize the five judgments:

Brand: Reputational Currency

Even before the first interaction occurs between two individuals, opinions are formed. If there is sufficient buzz or word of mouth about a person, that information quickly morphs into a reputation. If there is no information about the person, then *cultural stereotyping* causes the interviewer (in our example) to fill in the blanks based upon assumptions about the group the interviewee represents.

Personal Appeal: Physical Impact, Auditory Cues, and Distinguishing Markers

Next comes the moment of actual, face-to-face contact. At this point, superficial factors like appearance, perceived freshness, and sound weigh in—in that order—often occurring almost simultaneously. If there is something culturally distinguishing about the person, that data is unconsciously filed away as well. Some of these data points are a good indicator of workplace success and some of them are not.

Work Product: Tangible Output

By the time the hiring manager (in an interview situation) reaches the output or work product stage, four judgments have already been made. Two key takeaways: the candidate may never get a chance to show work product, due to the negative impact of the first four judgments; second, neither party (interviewer or candidate, in this example) may be aware of the strong, unconscious dynamics underpinning the surface interaction.

All Five Judgments culminate in the Orchid Effect. This is the categorization of an individual as being an orchid because they are unique and differentiated, as opposed to being rejected for the task or position because of diversity.

Secondary impact of the Five Judgments:

The impact of the five judgments does not end with the initial Orchid Effect. Based on the conscious and unconscious processes that occur, the judge (for example, the interviewer) also feels competent to assess:

- How "good" is this person? Positive, negative, neutral
- How potentially dangerous might he be *to my career* or the organization? High, medium, low
- At what level (relative to me) should I place this person mentally? Superior, peer, inferior

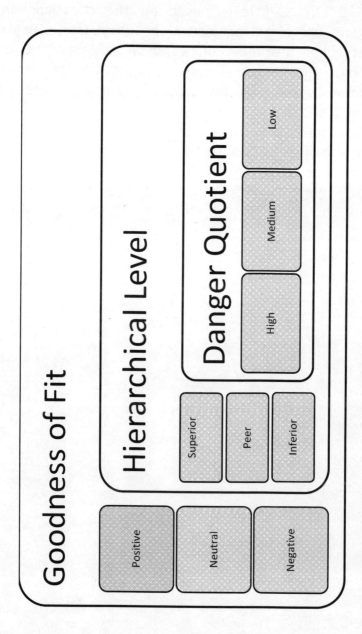

Figure 2: Impact on organizational fit, hierarchical level and danger quotient

Don't automatically jump to the conclusion that the interviewer will select the *positive, low danger, inferior* candidate for the Program Manager role we referenced.

The key is not to come up with a formulaic answer as to whom the interviewer will, or should, select. The objective is to transform the process so that unconscious snap judgments evolve into more conscious and balanced decisions.

Cost of Stereotyping in the Workplace:

Let me illustrate the very real cost of stereotyping in the workplace. Let's assume that we are interviewing candidates A and B for a Program Manager position, for a large, cross-functional international project.

The buzz is good about Candidate A—one of her friends is your marketing contact and recommended her. She is personable, well dressed, and well spoken. She exudes confidence and poise. She arrives on time for her interview and is knowledgeable about the latest World Cup, French Open, or Super Bowl (depending on which country this interview is taking place). She promises to send you an example of her last big program and the software tools she used after the interview is over.

Candidate B is an unknown quantity. She applied online through the company recruiting process. She is dressed neatly but not particularly smartly. Her English is good but her name is hard to pronounce. She has no perfume and you detect a mild, sweaty odor when you approach her. She is wearing a simple iron bangle that you can't help noticing, and you feel it's inappropriate for an interview situation. Also, her palms are clammy when you shake hands. You make a comment about the sporting event referenced earlier and she looks blankly at you. As you smile and exchange pleasantries you speculate that she has low social skills and is a little different. She pulls out a folder with some glowing references and a sample project plan, using new tracking software that you have not seen before. You note down the name of that software so you can give it to Candidate A later.

What just happened?

Somewhere between the third and fourth judgments, you made a selection decision that Candidate A would be a better Program Manager than Candidate B.

What happened is known as the Orchid Effect.

Based on mostly subjective decision-making processes, you also decided that Candidate A is a better organizational fit for the job. The Orchid Effect was negative for Candidate B. Based on cues such as lower physical appeal and lack of knowledge of current sporting events, you categorized her on the negative end of the spectrum: different enough to be rejected for the position.

When you selected Candidate A over Candidate B, did you make the right decision?

Possibly. However, there is a good chance that you made an incorrect, highly costly hiring decision based on factors not pertaining to the job at hand.

Let's analyze both the candidates using spider web charts depicting relative strengths and weaknesses for the position of Program Manager. This is a visual summary of the cost of stereotyping that is a result of the Five Judgments.

Candidate A	Score (on 10)
Reputational Currency	7
Physical Impact	6
Auditory Cues	6
Distinguishing Markers	6
Work Product	4

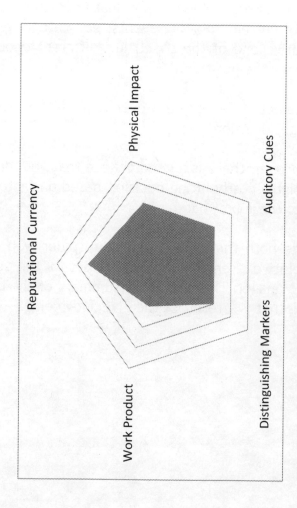

Figure 3 Cost of Stereotyping: Candidate A Selected

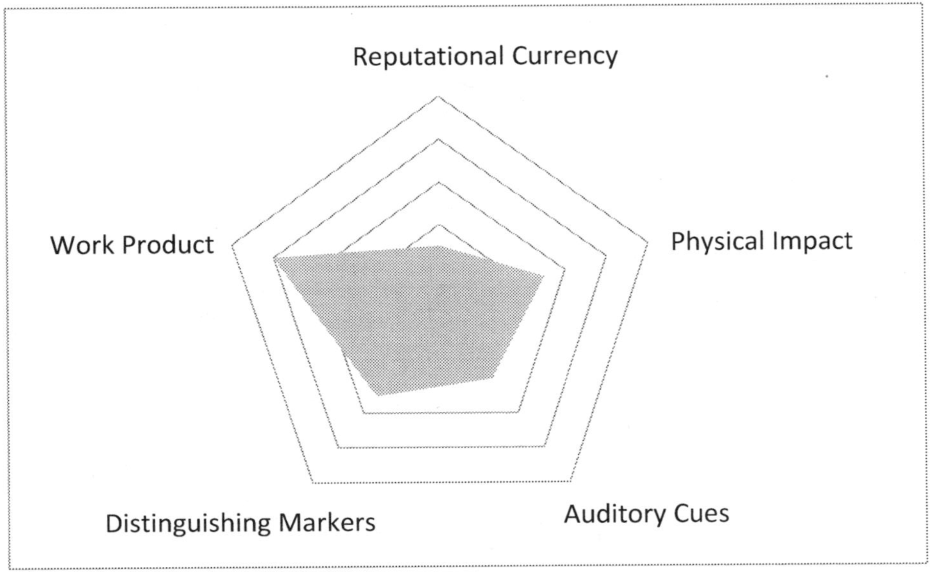

Candidate B	Score (on 10)
Reputational Currency	3
Physical Impact	5
Auditory Cues	4
Distinguishing Markers	5
Work Product	8

Figure 4 Cost of Stereotyping: Candidate B Rejected

Candidate B is rejected due to the first four judgments, though her work output may be higher.

Candidate A is selected for a program manager role due to a positive read on the first four judgments, though her work product, output and overall dollar value to organization may be lower than Candidate B.

The Orchid Effect, as a result of the five judgments, is that Candidate B is assessed as being too different and not a good fit for the organization.

Let us now overlay the two diagrams. This will give us a comparative visual, which relates to the very real cost of stereotyping in the workplace.

The difference between Candidate B and Candidate A's work products (8-4) is a proxy for the cost of stereotyping in the workplace.

The immediate cost of workplace stereotyping is reduced output or product quality. The long term cost of stereotyping is an unengaged workforce, with higher attrition, passive aggressive workplace behaviors and lower morale.

Author's note: While the book focuses on cultural diversity, obviously this is a multivariate analysis. Cultural stereotyping is not the only dynamic occurring here. Ageism or sexism (limiting beliefs about the abilities of females in technical areas, for example) may kick in as well. There is a propensity toward cultural stereotyping in each of the judgments (for example, the IIT engineer stereotype example in reputational currency, how ethnic a person looks in physical impact, and a foreign accent in auditory cues).

If there is only one page you bookmark in this book, let it be this page.

Project Manager Rating	A	B
Reputational Currency	7	3
Physical Impact	6	5
Auditory Cues	6	4
Distinguishing Markers	6	5
Work Product	4	8

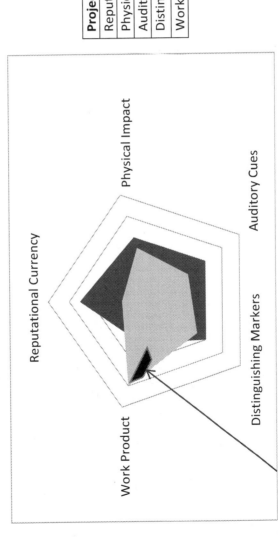

Figure 5 Comparative Work Product of Candidates A and B

Managing the orchid effect successfully as an interviewer:

Now that we understand the five judgments, let's say we are interviewing a culturally diverse candidate for the same Program Manager role. What are some things we can do to manage our orchid effect or tendency to reject people who are perceived as being negatively different from us?

- Be aware of cultural and other stereotypes from your self-assessment on limiting beliefs.
- Focus on the requirements for the role, and make 75 percent or more of the hiring decision based on those requirements.
- If possible, try to shake or displace the limiting beliefs that no longer apply.
- Changing limiting beliefs is difficult but possible over time with determination and will.

Be aware of cultural and other stereotypes from your self-assessment on limiting beliefs:

I know someone who had a strong bias against men with long hair. It was illogical, but a strongly held belief. What if this person were interviewing a turbaned man whose culture prohibits cutting of hair for religious reasons?

Focus on the requirements for the role:

Reverse the order of the judgments. If it's for a program manager role, be laser-sharp about what the job requirements are in terms of output. Make sure you cover those questions first. Get examples of work product. Use references to ask previous employers about output. Minimize the effect of superficial judgments. This applies to non-cultural stereotypes as well. A man who recognizes his susceptibility for hiring "sexy young things" may ask a sensible, older colleague to be part of an interview panel with him. *If you make 75 percent or more of the hiring decision based on tangible job requirements, will you not, over time, get a closer match for the role?* As you read this sentence, some of you are remarking, indignantly: There is nothing new in this; *that's what I always do.*

No, you don't.

Trust me on this one. If you are human, you don't.

If possible, try to shake or displace the limiting beliefs that no longer apply: This is the most difficult but typically the most rewarding aspect of taking a diversity foray. Feedback lies all around us, if we are only willing to receive it and then act on it. Sometimes we change our actions and then our beliefs follow suit. My advice: take

baby steps to change your limiting behaviors first. A simple action is taking the time to learn how a direct report pronounces his country's—or his own—name. (For example: *Iraq* is pronounced "E-Rahq" by people from that country, not "Eye-Rack.")

To summarize: Be aware of your biases, and how the superficial judgments may be clouding the accuracy of the orchid effect. Focus on what is required for the job, the role, and the project and give work content more importance than subjective opinions and feelings in the decision.

A simple tool to aid in this endeavor is to collect work product samples ahead of time and then focus interview questions on the work content.

The most powerful tool is self-awareness and the willingness to attempt self-management.

Managing the orchid effect successfully: interviewee

Two sets of behaviors will make for a successful interview. One is high level or strategic, around understanding and leveraging your brand and particularly distinguishing markers.

The second set of behaviors is tactical and practical.

Practical tips for making a good first interviewing impression:

- Add a jacket (or suit if it's a more formal situation).
- Always arrive twenty minutes early. If it's a complicated location, practice going there a day earlier; there may be one-way streets or excessive traffic.

- Sleep well the night before.
- Have a good shower and shampoo, and make sure your hair looks neat (stylish would be a bonus).
- Eat something nutritious and filling; carry a bottle of water with you.
- Carry extra copies of your resume on good quality paper.
- Have a dark folder (which at least looks like leather) or laptop bag (for women).
- Practice a good strong handshake.
- Have good eye contact with the interviewer.
- Be prepared: know company revenue, profitability, and head count numbers as a bare minimum.
- Come across as poised, and openly share your strengths without boasting.

In the section on cross cultural communication, we will discuss some more techniques that apply in all workplace situations, including interviews.

Chapter 8

Diversity Foray: a new model for cross cultural effectiveness

So far, we have explored the real costs of cultural stereotyping in the workplace.

Now, we come to a suite of tools for effectively improving our multi cultural competence. This *diversity foray* toolkit is divided into two segments: techniques that move us forward and responses to avoid.

If we consider a book to be a living organism, this chapter would be the brains.

When faced with knotty diversity issues, I started observing—over a period of two decades—that certain responses were highly effective, while others resulted in a complete breakdown in communications. In the positive case, leaders were able to work right past their differences and achieve an aggressive goal with mutual understanding and respect. On the negative side, it appeared that seemingly simple and lucrative deals were mishandled—key employees left organizations and unheeding comments resulted in costly lawsuits. Product lines were closed in promising new geographical locations due to the lack of mutual understanding.

I started developing a working list of diversity *do's* and *don'ts*. After twenty years, I took all the data and attempted an "engineering-principles-based" approach of data harvesting and pattern recognition. The resulting framework evolved into this **Diversity Foray** model, which has now been introduced to people from over twenty-three countries.

What is a Diversity Foray?

The Oxford Dictionary has several definitions of **foray**, one of which is "a spirited attempt to become involved in a new activity or sphere.". A foray is basically **a journey into unknown territory**: an exploration, if you will, where there is an element of both trust in self and faith in others—with an element of what David Whyte, the poet, refers to as "stepping out of the boat."

The elements of this original framework or model are:

- *Do:* Ask, Adapt, Accept, Appreciate (four A's morph into "foray" and the meaning fits well).
- *Don't*: Shun, Patronize, Assume, Crumble, Escalate.
- *Assess*: Your personal Brand, Biases, and Beliefs.

When we put all the pieces of the puzzle together effectively, we will experience cross cultural effectiveness that positively impacts our business performance. We are in a cusp stage in the world today. We have one arm stretched forward to the future—with emerging powers in new geographies and paradigms—while the other arm rests on past successes and current knowledge for stability. Looking back at the wisdom of the now distant twentieth century, we are poised to emerge stronger as one comprehensive global entity.

So I ask you, with optimism in my heart:

Shall we take a Diversity Foray together?

Figure 6: Diversity Foray Cyclical Flow and Tools

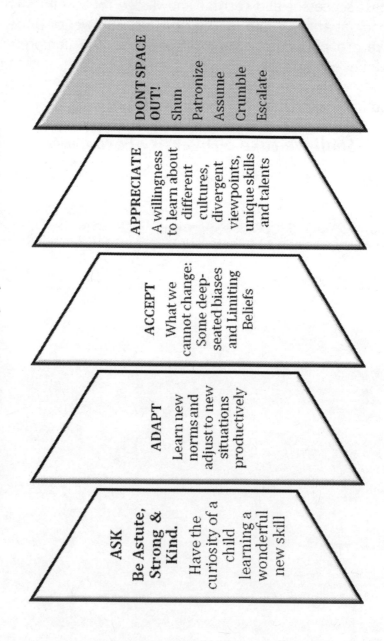

ASK
Be Astute, Strong & Kind.
Have the curiosity of a child learning a wonderful new skill

ADAPT
Learn new norms and adjust to new situations productively

ACCEPT
What we cannot change: Some deep-seated biases and Limiting Beliefs

APPRECIATE
A willingness to learn about different cultures, divergent viewpoints, unique skills and talents

DON'T SPACE OUT!
Shun
Patronize
Assume
Crumble
Escalate

Chapter 9

The Four A's: do Ask, Accept, Adapt, Appreciate

Let's now look at each of the elements of the model in a systematic manner.

- First we will explain the four A's of desirable responses when in a diversity situation.
- Next we explore negative diversity responses that derail us, hence: "don't SPACE out."
- Finally, we reexamine our own beliefs, brands, and biases (the self-assessment in Chapter 4).

When we (as an organization) put all the pieces together with emotional intelligence, we open the window to self-awareness, which can positively impact our productivity and global presence.

1. Do ASK:

Asking is critical to Diversity Awareness.

The simple word *ask* incorporates self-analysis and awareness, as well as a complex set of skills required when asking another person a question for maximum results. The first step is always self-analysis.

Using the self-assessment tools (brands, biases, and beliefs) ask yourself:

- What is my brand and presence?
- What are my biases and limiting beliefs?

Then we observe others and try (with their cooperation) to see points of difference and similarities in their approach to various aspects of culture—such as core values, religion, norms on hygiene, food, appearance, and relationships.

A key question in cross cultural effectiveness is:

"Does being different work for me or against me?"

The other aspect of asking is the topic of the conversation and the question being asked. This incorporates both the content and the *process*:

- *What* you want to know is the *content*.
- *How* you ask the person (in your journey of self-exploration) the diversity question is the *process*.

Well-meaning people regularly come to me for diversity advice because they are perplexed.

When they asked a caring diversity question (in their opinion), it was met with very negative, defensive, or hostile results.

The *how* refers to the way to ask questions so that you maintain others' self-esteem, as opposed to (often inadvertently) making people feel small by being patronizing, or just plain rude.

An easy way to remember the desired techniques for ASK is with the acronym:

- **A**stute
- **S**trong
- **K**ind

Let's illustrate this point with a style diversity example.

Trevor routinely has lunch at a restaurant that offers unlimited soup.

It's the main meal of his day, and he usually has three bowls.

Three different styles of waitperson ask Trevor if he wants the third bowl:

"Would you like another bowl of soup?"

Neutral, unless her eyes are raised or there's an emphasis on the word *another* . . . Perfectly fine.

"You're not going to have a *third* bowl of soup, are you?"

No humor, eyebrows raised, definitely judgmental, "You . . ." (Fill in negative word)

"Isn't this soup great? Have a third bowl . . . we have wheel barrows to take you out! ☺"

The third waitperson is a charming, humorous woman who was joking with Trevor and her other customers about lots of things. Genuinely pleasant, the wheel barrow comment was made in such a fun way that it was not offensive at all.

What's the key learning?

Who do you think Trevor tipped the least? (# 2 is indeed the correct response)

The most? In spite of, or maybe *because of* the wheel barrow comment and the humor, Trevor tipped # 3 the most—and he walked away smiling.

This is a case of an individual responding to three different behavioral styles having a direct monetary impact. Now, let's look at the business implications of this example. If we believe in customer service as a core value for our business, what can we learn from this style diversity example that applies to cross cultural effectiveness?

The key learning is the *immense power in the "art and heart of the ask"* resulting in higher work product or output.

To summarize:

- The key to asking effectively is *the place of caring* from which the question comes.
- While the words you use when asking the question are important, nonverbal communication is even more critical than dialogue.
- Be *authentic* to your style. If you're not humorous by nature, don't try to be funny—especially in a diversity situation. It will backfire badly.
- Let's do a quick reality check. Do you find yourself getting baffling results when you ask people from different cultures seemingly innocent questions? Is there a tension in the body language of the recipient?
- When learning how to use the ASK tool, answer these questions:
  - Will asking this question increase my diversity quotient?
  - Will it improve my relationship with the recipient of the question?
  - Is it possible that I will offend this person by asking this question?
  - What is it about this question that may be awkward or difficult for me?

- *By all means ask,* and take a few extra seconds to ask *better. And try not to assume.*

Another aspect of asking has to do with analysis.

When in a diversity scenario, it's good to have some frame of reference questions in the back of your mind.

How sensitive is this person?

In a 2007 *O, The Oprah Magazine* issue, Martha Beck references HDPs: *Highly Defensive People.*

- Let's follow the case of Olivia *(name changed for confidentiality; example is a combination of more than one person).*
- Olivia used to be an HDP.
- It was very hard to ask her a civil question, particularly if it were asked by one or two people. After working in this diversity space, Olivia observed a perceptible drop in defensiveness.
- An "aha" was that *the same question, asked by another person using the exact same words did not evoke a defensive response from Olivia.*
- Since the second person never sniped at Olivia in general, she was able to hear the question, in spite of being a defensive person at that time.
- Keep asking yourself good questions about your emotional responses in diversity situations.
- Increase your self-awareness and emotional intelligence, the way Olivia was able to.
- Ask the same questions about other people's emotional responses in diversity situations.
- Notice which people are easy to talk to and which are not.

- Ask yourself why some people who are different connect with you and some don't.

Maya Angelou said, "People will forget what you said, people will forget what you did, but people will never forget how you made them feel."

*How do you make people feel when **you** ask **them** tough diversity questions?*

*How do people make you feel when **they** ask **you** tough diversity questions?*

Ask whether *your* differences are holding you back in your career and personal life or making you a unique, valuable resource?

> *Olivia turned the corner when people at work (such as HR managers, functional vice presidents, consultants, and executive coaches) started calling her regularly and asking for her advice in sticky diversity situations. The more freely they related embarrassing events, came clean about faux pas, were real and candid, the more Olivia realized that she was now safe to ask questions, because she had moved from an HDP to an open listener. Her power and presence increased dramatically.*

- If our intent is pure, it partially offsets a lack of experience or skills.
- A lack of malice comes shining through as we ask the question.
- Diversity work is a bridging exercise that is 90 percent based on positive intent.
- When the person asking tries her best, and the person responding hears the thought openly and non-defensively, we are able to bridge the gaps between us.
- We are then able to have a real dialogue in which both parties learn something.

Yes, asking can be as powerful and simple as that.

In the August 23, 2012 Harvard Business Review blog, Bill Taylor makes an excellent case for the argument: *It's harder (and more important) to be kind than clever.* He gives examples from Amazon's Jeff Bezos, as well as the Panera Bread Company incident, which gained their store manager Suzanne Fortier (and the company) immense reputational currency. Brandon Cook's grandmother, sick in a hospital, craved Panera's clam chowder, Taylor recounts. When Panera made soup especially for her—as an act of kindness on a day it didn't usually make soup—word spread like wildfire through social media. The second point Taylor makes is that it is striking that "her simple gesture attracted such global attention and acclaim."

In diversity excellence, we allow ourselves to be kind when doing so is the right thing to do. We set aside the misconception that unkindness and loss of face is necessary for business success. In the workplace, people need respect and understanding now more than ever.

Who are the people who have treated you with kindness when you were in a particularly vulnerable situation? When it would have been only too easy to make you feel small and insignificant? We all have them, interestingly enough, since we are humans and not robots. Are these the leaders who garner your true followership? Or are you inspired by an autocratic manager who ridicules anyone who ventures outside his outdated norms?

I rest my case.

Remember the two key concepts are that there is an *art and heart of asking,* which is embodied in a simple acronym for "ask": *Astute *Strong *Kind.*

2. Do Accept:

Once you have uncovered some key differences between yourself and the other entity (the person, team, or country where you will do business) ask yourself, what are the things that you do not like and cannot easily change? What will you have to learn to live with?

Life is littered with situations that we learn to accept. In diversity work, due to our self-serving biases, each person in a dialogue may feel that the burden of acceptance is falling upon him.

We give up on certain things after carefully weighing the pros and cons of the situation.

A logical heuristic to help make the *accept decision* is to apply a simple cost benefit analysis.

- Is this fight worth fighting?
- Is this something that is important enough to try to change?
- How much energy will I spend, and what will the payoff be?

Another area that usually falls into the *accept* category is having deep-rooted assumptions about values, appearance, and hygiene.

Accept example during United States-Europe business trip:

Jim and a direct report, Bonnie, were on a business trip, traveling from the United States to the Schengen states. Being culturally sensitive, Jim was embarrassed by some of the comments that Bonnie was throwing around at a dinner hosted by their European customers. Bonnie, a stickler for hygiene, was very vocal in her comments about the "gross bathroom" in the hotel, offensive smells, the inadequacy of hotel room cleaning processes, restaurant food being served on dirty plates, and so forth. Twice, Jim observed strong negative non-verbal reactions from their European clients when Bonnie loudly expressed disgust for "filthy habits" in front of them.

Jim took Bonnie aside and said, firmly but gently:

"Bonnie, you are welcome to carry your own hand sanitizer and do whatever makes you comfortable. At the same time, can you accept the reality that the thousands of people who live in this city will not change their practices because of your comments? And we really need this contract."

There are many things one has to accept—some on a daily basis—when one chooses to live, or work in (or with) another country.

You may have a strong negative reaction to this statement. That will be an indicator of learning capability to me. *A respectful, thoughtful difference of opinion must, on occasion, exist between reader and author.* That will mean that independent thought processing is occurring. And that **you are reading and processing the book,** instead of just leafing through the pages.

The United States has been a *rewarding and empowering* home for over twenty-six years.

Yet, I must *accept* that every few months an incident will occur which calls on every ounce of available "diversity gracefulness." Last week during a business workshop, the presenter showed a funny video about fast food orders; the video had an offensive punch line regarding a heavily accented Indian call center employee. My diversity choice was to *accept* the awkward situation without comment. Living by choice in a place where my country's stereotypes are a certain way makes me a target every now and then. It's often not personal. And . . . when it *is* personal, I have tools to deal with it.

Hopefully, when you finish reading this book, you will know these tools and be able to apply them.

But we must **accept the costs that come with benefits**. The benefits of living in the United States are tremendous, and for me they far outweigh the occasional stereotypical jab that is part of the equation.

3. Do Adapt:

Adapting refers to the ability to flex according to the situation. It does not mean caving in and doing something that goes against your values just to buy peace. Often, diversity work can seem like tightrope walking. It is difficult to adapt without knowing what people's hot buttons are. *Be aware of your own response, and beliefs* before deciding the extent to which you are willing to adapt. When we try to make two opposing viewpoints coincide, we cannot both stay without movement at two different ends of a spectrum. A valuable tool is the power to adapt—to be flexible, to adjust based on new data or insights.

Once you have uncovered some key differences between yourself and the other entity (the person, team, or country in which you will do business) ask yourself: *what are the things that I do not like but can **adapt** to?*

Example: Punctuality adaptation in the Middle East:

You manage a large multinational company (MNC) based in Japan and will be starting operations in the Middle East. When you arrive for your first face-to-face interaction with a key potential customer in Dubai, the meeting does not start on time. There are lavish snacks and the meeting room is beautiful. Forty-five minutes later, the leader's administrative assistant comes in with an obviously false reason for the leader's delay. You are scrupulously punctual—you consider getting to a meeting five minutes early as being a little late—and yet you need the business!

There are many norms we cannot change, but if we understand them (especially if it is a norm from another culture) we can *adapt* to them.

Viable adaptation strategies include:
- Occupying oneself for a few minutes with reading materials
- Mentally rehearsing so temper does not spill out into the meeting
- Deliberately coming to meetings thirty minutes later than the scheduled time

Sometimes people think they are adapting by completely ignoring their own point of view.

They blindly comply with everything suggested by the person in the cultural mainstream.

This is not adapting in the pure sense; this is suppressing.

Over time, suppressing leads to anger, frustration, and disappointment. Truly adapting is a more self-aware way of responding.

4. Do Appreciate:

The most powerful results occur when we become aware of our respective viewpoints, ask powerful questions to truly understand points of reference, and then appreciate the learning that occurs from this diversity. The person with a culturally diverse viewpoint can open our eyes to a whole new world.

For example, different cultures have dramatically opposing views as to the value of the elderly. In multiple cultures across the world, people become invisible after they turn sixty. If, rather than follow this approach blindly we instead *appreciate* people from another culture who treat the elderly as valuable resources, we may even try it out ourselves. We may ask our parents to share stories of their childhood with our children in order to transfer precious legacy knowledge of our roots.

The difference between adapting and appreciating is that one usually adapts to a difference that one doesn't like. Appreciation has to do with a difference that you find more positive than negative.

To summarize, the four A's of the diversity foray are:

- Ask
- Adapt
- Accept
- Appreciate

Chapter 10

Don't SPACE (Shun, Patronize, Assume, Crumble, Escalate) out

"Don't SPACE out" is a simple way to remember what *not to do* in a difficult diversity situation. Remember, in a high stress business situation, tempers may be running high, and our brains may not be the part in control.

The acronym I use is SPACE as in "Don't space out."
Don't . . .

- **S**hun: Avoid, walk or run away from, ostracize
- **P**atronize: Condescend, make the other person feel small, marginalize
- **A**ssume: Jump to conclusions, based on (often unconscious) limiting and stereotypical beliefs
- **C**rumble: Believe a diverse person's false or outrageous statement blindly, acquiesce too easily
- **E**scalate: Make things worse than they are by overreacting

Don't Shun:

There may be many things we don't approve of when working with people from different cultures, religion, value systems, or ethnicities. Shunning people because they are different is very common. In extreme forms, this is the basis of deep-seated prejudice and bias.

- Common *shunning* statements are things like "we don't mix with x, y, or z people."
- "Stay away from _____ if you don't want to be robbed."

Please don't misunderstand me. Obviously I am not suggesting we wander, Pollyannaish, into a dangerous part of town just to show we are culturally liberal. My basic assumption is that we are exercising a good dose of common sense and self-preservation, and not putting ourselves in any physical or emotional risk by undertaking this Diversity Foray.

Don't Patronize *(or allow yourself to be patronized):*

People from developed nations often make blanket assumptions about people from third world countries. An indicator that patronizing might be occurring is the phrase *you people*. When you notice patronizing comments, a powerful technique that works wonders is one simple word:

"Ouch!"

Last week, in a room full of professionals, Wesley jokingly made a comment about whether someone called Juanita could understand English. I looked at Wesley and said, calmly and firmly, "Ouch!" Patronizing other cultures often happens subconsciously. Our objective is to assist the misguided offender in increasing his self-awareness, without getting emotionally invested. Also, always keep the possibility open that this type of comment—though it may have come across as patronizing—was not intended to be so; perhaps there were mitigating circumstances.

A very common location for patronizing is the company break room. People from other cultures routinely cringe when bizarre news items from another country are brought out as gospel truth and as a norm for that country. This includes things like "Wow, do they really eat *frogs' legs*? I heard about it in the news!" followed by the patronizing comment, "Lee, I am sure *you* don't do this!"

Poor Lee: caught between a rock and a hard place.

If there is one Lee out there whom this book can help, equip, or train . . . then that will be time well spent.

So, if you are Lee, what should you do?

1. Understand whether the comment's intent is to hurt you or is a genuine request for information.
2. Assess your emotional state at that moment.
3. If you find yourself having a visceral response while listening, do not say anything that you will regret later.
4. Don't get defensive, regardless of your choice of response.
5. If you are able to come up with a crisp, coherent response to the comment, do so.
6. Ahead of time, practice some good answers to repeated questions, and have them available to be pulled out in situations like this.
7. Don't crumble under pressure by either apologizing or babbling.
8. Stay true to your presence and brand while maintaining your poise.

Some phrases tend to cause additional anger and resentment and must be avoided. If a comment includes a damaging phrase like *one of us, you people* or *people like you*, it moves the error from slightly annoying to highly offensive patronizing. For example, if your boss says, "Marissa, I am so impressed by your English! You must have worked hard to *sound like one of us* . . ." then you will not easily excuse or forgive her.

Guidelines to authentically deal with tough (patronizing) diversity situations:

➢ First of all, be sure you're not being an HDP (highly defensive person) and super sensitive to comments that are *not* patronizing.
➢ If you are certain it is a patronizing comment, decide your choice of *presence*:

  ○ Firm while making a point
  ○ Mature and quiet
  ○ Authentically annoyed
  ○ Emotional, no holds barred, no political correctness
  ○ Calm and courageous
  ○ Other choices authentic to you . . . the key point being, make a *choice* not a knee-jerk reaction

➢ Depending on what you chose as appropriate, point it out.
➢ If not (you have to choose which battles to pick) . . . let it go.
➢ And, more importantly, make sure *you* aren't the one consciously or unconsciously patronizing others.

Author's note:

While I have elaborated the steps involved in choosing your "presence" and acting according to it in the "patronize" section, this awareness and choice of response is a powerful diversity tool for almost every aspect of your Diversity Foray.

Don't Assume:

If there is **one** thing you walk away with after reading this book, let it be this:

Do not make blind assumptions! In diversity work this is absolutely critical. There is no end to the assumptions we make—on a daily basis.

Do not assume that:

- People from other countries are superior because they have lighter skin
- People with higher SAT scores are smarter than you
- People who wear new designer clothes are classier than those who shop at thrift stores
- People in mansions with swimming pools are happier than people in crowded apartments
- People who can't speak French are *petite bourgeoisie*
- Someone who doesn't laugh at your jokes doesn't have a sense of humor; what else might be the reason?

The list is never ending.

A good way to combat assumption mania: **Ask.**

The best way: **Ask skillfully**!

Don't Crumble:

People crumble under pressure, hiding strongly held beliefs and positions until the emotional disconnect and tension of this weakness become unbearable.

Then they either leave the organization or—in extreme situations—have a nervous breakdown,.

If someone says to a strict vegetarian, "We are going to a Japanese restaurant where the main focus is eating sushi and we are ordering for the group," don't crumble and say "That's fine" if it makes you uncomfortable. Be respectful and make sure your needs are known. People who respect themselves find it easy to state their point of view with poise.

In 2012, the *Harvard Business Review* printed a great article about what adds up over time to happiness and unhappiness in interactions. Surprisingly, they found that a larger number of *small* interactions over time led to more unhappiness than a few large fights or issues.

If we consistently crumble under perceived pressure (which may be felt by us, even when there is no pressure exerted by another person) and have no sense of identity, over time we will be conscious of a constant, numb feeling. This feeling, in turn, will morph into the limiting belief: *I'm not good enough*. This damages everyone.

We are consistently more productive in an environment where we feel respected and understood (regardless of whether the other person *agrees or disagrees* with us).

Now let's approach this phenomenon from a different perspective. People from the underrepresented group (whatever that group might be) sometimes use what is called the *race card* to manipulate the truth. In other words, they get special treatment by lying about their cultural boundaries. When they do this, well-meaning people "crumble" as an act of consideration of the special needs of the underrepresented group.

I have heard many ridiculous things under the guise of "We don't do this in our culture."

Unfortunately, there are two negative consequences of this behavior. It hurts both the mainstream population as well as the diverse group.

How?

When the lie/deception/misuse of diversity is found out (which happens very often), then the person that crumbled feels misused and trust is broken. The next time someone else from that diverse group is in a similar situation, they are no longer given the benefit of the doubt. The person who used the race card tarnishes them with the same brush.

Crumbling under false pretenses: school holidays example:

> Parents from an Asian country who were living in the United State took their daughter out of school on the pretext that it was a "religious holiday in our culture." The school, wanting to appear culturally inclusive, granted the child the day off which she then used to play hooky with her parents.
>
> What will happen when the school discovers the ruse?
>
> A person from another culture—who has genuine religious holidays—will suffer.
>
> The child, learning that lying is a good use of diversity, will most likely play the race card as an adult.
>
> The school principal will feel betrayed and, unconsciously or consciously, will have a bias or prejudice (perhaps a harsh stereotype) of people from that culture.

From day-to-day tasks (for example, *Elisa comes from a culture where people don't return phone calls or e-mails, so we just have to accommodate her*) to long-term, physically damaging modes of behaving (for example, *men from this culture don't do chores at home because it's their culture*)—good, kind-hearted people crumble under pressure and cave in, even when their instincts suggest they hold firm. And when they do, it's a travesty for many reasons:

- It's unfair to the rest of the world who doesn't get special *get out of jail free* passes.

- When we allow a few diverse people to play the race card, we make it harder for hardworking, gifted, culturally diverse people to be accepted. They get tainted because someone tried to take advantage of the system.
- Using the race card is a form of lying or manipulation; transmitting these values to future generations is just wrong.

Don't Escalate:

Finally we come to the most dangerous of all the diversity errors: escalation—taking a small incident or difference and making it hugely damaging by fanning the fires. For centuries, wars have been fought on the basis of religious differences, and we are all painfully aware that this issue continues to exist worldwide. A single person or group of persons with ideological differences of opinion can *escalate* situations, creating havoc in the process. September 11th is, unfortunately, all we have to say for this point to be made.

> In August 2012 in Wisconsin, a lone gunman entered a *Gurudwara* (Sikh place of worship) and opened fire on helpless and innocent men, women, and children.
>
> When interviewed, neighbors and acquaintances of the gunman had no idea this person was so prejudiced.
>
> As a point of reference, traditionally, Sikh men wear turbans. (Their religion prohibits them from cutting their hair, so the men wear turbans as a practical way to manage their hair.)
>
> The gunman (who I will not honor by naming) apparently mistook the turban as a sign of religious terrorism, and so killed six people before taking his own life.

This is why this book is so important. Bias and racial prejudice walk hidden amongst us.

What we can do to *combat this rising storm of racial escalation* is to **stop the madness**, one person at a time.

And that starts with the people we can truly impact most of all, ourselves.

Remember the Michael Jackson song and line: "I'm talking to the Man in the Mirror . . .	I'm asking him to change his ways . . .	If you want to make the world a better place . . . *change!"*

Guidelines for defusing an escalating situation:

- Self-awareness is, once again, the first prerequisite for combating escalation.
- When you feel like things are getting out of hand, *do not escalate if you are able to control yourself.*
- Exercise the freedom of choice that you possess by postponing or canceling the meeting, event, or confrontation until you are able to be rational and *de-escalate* emotionally. It will be one of the smartest things you have done, for all parties involved.

Key Learning: Section Two

➤ The five judgments propose an original framework to understand cultural stereotyping in the workplace.
➤ They are:
  ○ Reputational Currency
  ○ Physical Impact
  ○ Auditory Cues
  ○ Distinguishing Markers
  ○ Work Product
➤ The five judgments accumulated equal the *Orchid Effect*: the person is either accepted as valuably different (a rare orchid), or not valued as an orchid and instead just rejected for being different.
➤ Subjective and costly business decisions brought on by diversity stereotyping result in productivity losses in the workplace.
➤ Being aware of the five judgments can reduce the cost of cultural stereotyping.
➤ Diversity work resides mainly in the gut and the heart, not in the head.
➤ The Diversity Foray is a simple set of guiding principles to increase effectiveness in diversity situations.
➤ The Diversity Foray has four A's (hence "Foray"): Ask, Adapt, Accept, Appreciate.
  ○ Ask questions authentically and carefully, first about yourself (your prejudices, biases, brand, and presence) and then others (watching content, tone of voice, and intent).
  ○ Adapt to cultural differences that you don't like.
  ○ Accept the differences that will not change (or are not worth the energy required).
  ○ Appreciate the beauty of our unique differences; perfection is not the goal here.

➤ Don't SPACE out: Shun, Patronize, Assume, Crumble, or Escalate.
➤ Use the Diversity Foray framework to function more rationally, even if emotions rush to your head.
➤ Strive to take back your *power of choice* when in an uncomfortable diversity situation.
➤ Be mindful of your brand and presence and act accordingly.

Section Three

Examining the Five Judgments

Analyzing the quantitative and qualitative costs of stereotyping at the workplace

Energy cannot be created or destroyed,
but it can be changed.

First Law of Thermodynamics

Chapter 11

Reputational Currency

Do you have any *buzz* that precedes your walking into the situation? For example, when you go into an interview, has someone you worked with already impressed upon the interviewer what a strategic thinker you are?

If you are looking for a job, keep in mind that people you have interacted with will receive calls or e-mails to ask about your fit for a specific role. They may be former colleagues, team members, or clients. Some of these people will deliver very specific, job dependent, unbiased positives and negatives, based on the requirements of a particular role. And some will just authoritatively give very arbitrary feedback about you based on minimal thought and supporting data points. It will just be based on your buzz or overall reputation.

Be very careful about the bridges you burn. An otherwise emotionally stable employee, Vera, was upset at being laid off unexpectedly. She sent an inflammatory e-mail to hundreds of people prior to leaving the organization. Vera didn't just burn bridges at that organization. Word spread like wildfire throughout the city, and—indeed further, and to this day—when you mention Vera, people say, "Oh, yes, remember that e-mail?"

Reputational currency is worth its weight in gold.

Real life example:

When Penelope Howard started out as an independent consultant, many people warned her about how tough it was to get business in this economy. Within a few months, Penelope had so much business that she started turning down or referring out most new clients. Why?

Because her reputational currency and buzz was solid. Her ex-bosses, colleagues, friends, and mentors:

- *Let prospective clients know she was available*

- *Called her before a round of interviews started for a coaching assignment*

- *Got her certified in their assessment and training tools*

- *By word of mouth, recommended her for any consulting or executive coaching projects, even giving their cell phone numbers for reference verification*

- *Sent Penelope RFPs for their companies' services (as some were in other organizations), unasked*

- *Invited her to dinners with CEOs*

- *Wrote glowing recommendations and endorsed her on LinkedIn*

- *Were, in short, her 40-person marketing team*

All of that translated to immediate business for Penelope, with zero marketing expense.

This occurred in spite of the presence of ten thousand coaches and consultants in Penelope's city.

Never underestimate the power of reputational currency. It physically translates to money in the bank.

What if you don't have any personal brand established yet?

That is when cultural stereotypes come into play.

If you don't know what a person stands for as an individual, you start extrapolating what that person may be like based on the group you perceive them to be a part of.

Reputational currency, in the absence of specific feedback about a person, moves into a predisposition—either positive or negative—toward a larger unit, even before the first meeting.

- We continually make assumptions based on insufficient data.
- We fill in reputational currency interpretations because of cultural biases and other stereotyping.
- Our low quality, subjective decisions translate to millions in opportunity costs at work.
- We pass over competent, qualified people for technical jobs, because we believe they (as part of their cultural group) are dishonest, from a "bad" religion, or for similarly arbitrary reasons—for example, predispositions from a name (John versus Juan).

Chapter 12

Physical Impact

Physical Impact	How attractive do you appear?	Physical characteristics: Is your face attractive? What is your weight range? How is your physique and hair?
		Apparel and accessories: judged based on perceived expensiveness equated with quality, style, and trendiness.
		Age grouping: young, middle aged, old.
		Do you smell fresh or do you have body odor? Is there something repellent about you?

Study after study show that a person's physical appearance has a disproportionately significant impression on how others view them on unrelated characteristics. I divide physical impact into two categories: *visual appeal* and *perceived freshness*.

Your **visual appeal** is a composite of *physical characteristics* and apparel, combined with your style index, age range, and overall appearance.

Physical characteristics start with what nature gave us: face, height, and general build. Arbitrary judgments are made about a person's weight and age range as well. How old do you appear to be? There is a *Goldilocks* phenomenon to age—*too old* and *too young* versus *just right* is defined subconsciously based on past experiences.

Should a fifty-year-old man dye his hair before going on an interview? Whatever our opinions may be on this subject, we cannot ignore how powerful one's visual appeal is in the context of business success.

Beauty, while being skin deep, assuredly lies in the eye of the beholder. That is where the cultural component becomes critical: *we make assumptions as to what visual appeal means based on our filters and values.* If Sara's messaging from childhood is that *a woman with short hair looks masculine,* she will wear long hair in a simple ponytail. This in turn will impact her perceived visual appeal to Josephine, whose subconscious belief is that *a long ponytail looks dowdy at work.*

The second key aspect of visual appeal has to do with *apparel and style*: what you wear, and how you wear it. Clothes, shoes, briefcases for men, purses for women, and hairstyles for both genders. All of these add up to subconscious messages about quality and trendiness.

If your reputational currency was initially positive, chances are there will be more leniency toward your visual impact than if your buzz was negative prior to first contact. That is part of a human heuristic where *we downplay conflicting data points in order to reduce dissonance in our brains*.

Freshness factors: In addition to visual appeal, *freshness* is a key component within this judgment. In other words: how clean and crisp do we appear? This subset of physical impact is overlooked the most when we talk about leveraging cultural diversity in the workplace.

Body odor is an unspoken yet critical part of the five judgments and is assigned the most importance in the United States. How fresh (and, by extrapolation, how clean) a person is, is primarily judged based on how they smell. An absence of odor is typically seen as neutral or positive. Too much perfume is frowned upon but not considered a huge negative (unless it's attar or musk, which subconsciously connects to a *misfit* characterization). Body odor is even worse; unfortunately, most leaders find it very tough to talk to their employees about this. This is a pity because this issue may manifest itself in unfortunate, more dramatic situations. For example, the person may have just boarded a flight but be forced to deplane due to body odor—a traumatic and only too real issue that occurs routinely in certain countries.

Regional food odors for Eastern Asia are strongly felt. Whether a perfume or deodorant is overpowering, pleasant, or inappropriate for the occasion, it is a highly subjective judgment, dependent on one's cultural background.

Let's say you are a functional leader of a multinational company. Your Canadian human resources (HR) manager calls you for advice about a dilemma she is struggling with. There is a high potential, high performing employee from Kenya who has strong body odor. Coworkers have started leaving hints for her by anonymously leaving deodorants and perfume at her desk. Your HR manager calls you for advice. Before reading this book, you may have assumed that this was a really minor issue, and since the employee is such a good performer, it was not worth reacting to. You will actually do the employee a favor by addressing this issue with directness and respectful honesty.

Freshness factors are uniquely critical in multi cultural competence and should be managed appropriately. It's not just about how the person smells. There are other conclusions that are subconsciously made about the person's overall cleanliness, sense of hygiene, and overall *goodness of fit* in an organization, based on one allegedly insignificant data point. A culturally diverse person, coming from an environment where freshness is not a critical factor (or hard to come by, for practical reasons), may have no idea of the negative physical impact this is having on her chances of fitting in.

To summarize, some of the key Physical Impact factors are:

- Your attractiveness
- Your age range
- Your clothes and accessories
- Your perceived freshness
- Your sense of style
- Your ethnic quotient
- Your perceived confidence level

In addition to judgments forming based on the viewer's perception of how rich, confident, and attractive you are, there is a predisposition to place this person at a certain level in a notional organization chart.

Chapter 13

Auditory cues

Here's a challenge: speak to a skilled behavioral professional for less than one minute. She will be able to assess your auditory impact at work, within a reasonable degree of accuracy. Add some details about your specific job title, role, and work environment, and the estimate will be even better—*in just one minute*. Coaches and consultants are routinely brought into organizations to increase the executive presence or *role readiness* of senior leaders, and some of the focus is purely to improve their auditory messaging.

Key auditory cues:

- Do they speak too fast?
  - What is *too fast*? The answer may depend on the culture in which one grew up. Too fast in Japan would probably be ridiculously slow in Israel.

- How high pitched is the voice?
  - High-pitched voices tend to command less respect than deep tones command.

- How does the person respond to humor?
  - Giggling, a loud guffaw, a delicate smile?

- What kind of words do they use?
  - Long or arcane word usage (notice how I deliberately used *arcane* here?) signals *erudite and well educated* in some cultures, but *stuffy and boring* in others.

- How fluent are they?
  - Do they struggle to find the correct word? If English is our second language, we first think in our mother tongue, then translate that word back into the English equivalent. This process takes time and impacts fluency.

- What is the strength and timbre of the person's voice?
  - Quivering tones and saying *umm*, or *I think*—versus strong, confident, *it is so* statements. The impressions these make on others are like night and day.

As mentioned earlier, put experienced, skilled behavioral professionals in the back of a staff meeting for about a minute while a leader is speaking to assess the impact of sound cues on the audience. You may be surprised at the results.

Here's the interesting part. Whereas the reputational currency factor largely related to judgments of values, competence, or goodness of fit for the organization, visual impact and auditory cues signal another dimension as well.

In addition to how we look, how we sound leads to an initial measure of power and hierarchy relative to the reviewer.

There is a subconscious placement of the person as being a superior, a peer, or below us in organizational hierarchy. You may have heard the term *gravitas* being used. If you are lucky enough to receive this accolade, it means you have been perceived positively on multiple judgments. This includes an ***executive presence*** (though you don't have to be an executive in an organization to have an executive presence), which includes how you look, sound, and smell as well as your overall poise and demeanor. You are a force to be reckoned with. That is your buzz.

Chapter 14

Distinguishing Markers

Throughout this book, we have asked a simple question: *is being different working for you or against you?*

A *Distinguishing Marker* is a feature that is unique to us. In marketing, we define product appeal in the context of its *unique selling proposition* (USP). In molecular biology, we define a genetic marker in terms of a DNA identifier. Now, synthesizing the two concepts, I introduce the term *Distinguishing Marker* in the context of business diversity.

A *Distinguishing Marker* is something that stands out and makes you memorable. There is real value to thoroughly comprehending the *ramifications of this concept in diversity work*. We can be seen as *different because we are rare orchids* or *different because we aren't valued or don't fit in.*

Distinguishing Marker Characteristics:

1. A distinguishing marker in one society may be completely insignificant in another.
2. A distinguishing marker is not an absolute. One's perception of how different one is, in this characteristic, is as important as the factor itself.

3. A distinguishing marker's impact depends on the relative exposure of the second party interacting with the person who has the marker.
4. A distinguishing marker may be physical, behavioral, or contextual.
5. We all have distinguishing markers.

Now let's examine each characteristic in more detail:

1. **A distinguishing marker in one society is not necessarily one in another, for the same person:** Imagine a woman in a black burka (traditional Muslim garb) walking in the streets of Paris, France. I choose this example because it is highly publicized and has huge levels of emotion attached to it. Based on the controversy, the speeches by politicians, and the news coverage, you can be sure that the burka is a distinguishing marker for Farida as she walks down Champs-Elysées. Put the same Farida in Saudi Arabia, and she literally melts into the background in a sea of black burkas.

2. **A distinguishing marker is not an absolute. The person's perception of how different she is, in this characteristic, is as important as the factor itself.** Let's say you have two friends, Jessica and Farida, both females who are six feet tall. Farida will reference her height within fifteen minutes of your interaction with her. For Jessica, height almost never comes up; it's a non-issue in her mind. The interesting phenomenon is that when you see Farida, you will almost always describe her as *that tall woman*—much more so than in Jessica's case.

3. **A distinguishing marker's impact depends on the relative exposure of the second party interacting with the person who has the marker.** Let's continue with Farida's example. If you are raised in Saudi Arabia and are now in Ireland, and Farida comes to interview for a position, you will notice that the burka looks more unusual in Ireland than the way slacks and a jacket look. However, you will—from your childhood exposure to the concept of burkas—be quite familiar with the item itself. Therefore, your frame of reference also helps determine the strength of a distinguishing factor.

4. **A distinguishing marker may be physical, behavioral, or contextual.** Let's say Farida is *wearing a burka*, and also happens to be *six feet tall*. Depending on whether you are meeting her in *Saudi Arabia or in Ireland*, you may focus on either of the two factors. If Farida happens to *interrupt your Senior Vice President constantly*, then you will forget her height and burka and you will just focus on this behavior.

5. **We all have distinguishing markers.** Let's be mindful of which of our distinguishing markers are working for us and which are working against us—in a specific context. Distinguishing markers have an element of genetic markers in that some of them come from our birth family. From a very young age, we learn behaviors that are approved and those that are not considered appropriate.

I have observed an unfortunate distinguishing marker in culturally diverse people from many countries, and that is ***the tendency to dominate group interactions***. I have personally observed this phenomenon in men and women from multiple countries. While we will illustrate techniques for giving feedback to someone about this issue in Section Five (Chapter 20, Feedback Skills), let's understand *the business ramification in the context of distinguishing markers*.

Let's say a woman is extremely bright, a strategic thinker, and has a lot to offer the organization. During the course of a daylong internal training workshop, she speaks out twenty-seven times in the larger group. She does so by either asking the instructor questions or by answering his questions. The norm is two or three times per person; the next most vocal person speaks only ten times.

By noon, other participants are rolling their eyes and have started tuning her out. This, therefore, is her distinguishing marker. If one of these people is asked to take her on his team for a plum assignment, what are the chances that he will want to?

The saddest part of the story is that this woman, who has a lot to offer, leaves the workshop convinced that people were impressed with her knowledge and abilities. Her distinguishing markers could have been brilliance and strategic thinking. It is critical that we learn to manage our distinguishing markers.

Also, distinguishing markers have an element of marketing's *unique selling proposition* if we are self-aware and look for patterns in feedback we receive from others.

How do you recognize a person's distinguishing markers at work?

Listen for the cues about Wesley's, Roberto's, and Sheila's distinguishing markers:

- Clarice in Accounting remarks, "Wesley can remember each and every profit and loss statement for our division for the last six years!"
- June in Marketing comments, "For a first year advertising agency executive, Roberto has over a dozen client interviews. How does he do it?"
- Martin in Human Resources complains, "Sheila is wearing inappropriately transparent shirts again, in spite of clear guidelines in our company dress code manual . . . What am I going to do with her?"

Let's say you are a typical office employee with a *combination of both negative and positive distinguishing markers*:

- You are highly committed and always follow through on projects; your word is your bond.
- You are as immature emotionally as you are strong technically.
- When people question your judgment or challenge your opinions, you tend to lose your temper and overreact.
- You don't have good fashion sense and wear outdated clothes.
- You are a kind and caring individual.
- You are extremely shy and introverted.

Which of your distinguishing markers would you like your boss to remember about you? And what can you do to manage his impressions?

To summarize:

- The fourth judgment has to do with our unique features, which are known as Distinguishing Markers.
- A Distinguishing Marker is real and powerful, and may come in many forms.
- People are often unaware of what their Distinguishing Marker is.
- Recognizing one's most powerful Distinguishing Marker is the first step to understanding this judgment.
- The next step is managing this phenomenon, particularly if it may derail your career.
- Culturally diverse employees, in particular, must understand the potential long-term career impact of this characteristic.
- Building one's brand based on a positive Distinguishing Marker is a strategic choice that we often overlook.
- While managing this Distinguishing Marker is important, staying authentic is even more so.

Chapter 15

Work Product

Do you find it interesting that we are coming to work product so late in this section?

As a reminder, when we refer to *work product*, we are talking about our tangible, measurable output. What is the product or service that we provide at work? If we are in an engineering function, our work product could be a design or a bridge. If we are organizational leaders, our work product or output may be revenue or profitability. Basically, work product or output is what we are—or will be—measured on at our performance review.

If a hiring manager really wants the best hire for the program manager role we referenced, she must first be aware of the five judgments, and how subjective the first four are. Next, she must examine her own cultural stereotypes and limiting beliefs. If she would focus on receiving examples of the candidates' work product, and speak specifically with references on output-related topics, chances are that output will be the deciding factor, as it should be.

Cost of Cultural Stereotyping: reduced output or product quality

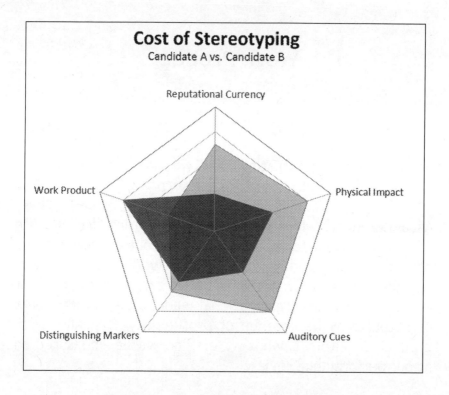

Figure 7: The cost of stereotyping
The difference between the two work products (8-4)
shows the cost of stereotyping

Remember the interview situation we discussed in the previous section?

Candidate A had great buzz, physical impact, and was well spoken, but has a low level of output or work product (4) whereas B, with a higher productivity level, or work product (8), was not so personable. When we selected A over B, we did the organization a disservice. The spider web above showcases the organizational cost of cultural stereotyping.

Hopefully, over time, the interviewer will be able to hire more consistent *8*s versus *4*s in terms of work product, which will, of course lead to higher workforce productivity. Especially for a program manager role, if one is aware of what is needed in order to be successful, then one is less likely to be biased.

Chapter 16

Synthesis of the Five Judgments: the Orchid Effect

If we synthesize the five judgments, we have the orchid effect.

Quick mental inventory of Cultural Fit, Level, Danger	**The Orchid Effect: Are you a rare find?** Our mind tends to confirm its initial reaction, unless unusual experiences (impressive vocabulary, crass rudeness) override first impressions. What is this person's potential place in the hierarchy? Trustworthiness? Cultural fit?	Based on the composite of the five judgments, an overall placement occurs. The person is now categorized within certain parameters as far as the 'judger' is concerned.

There is a specific reason that I called this the Orchid Effect. When you are different, do people see you as rare and valuable like the orchid? Are they then willing to make an effort to understand you and what it takes for you to thrive in a different environment? Or are you seen as annoyingly different, and not worth the high maintenance?

When someone is culturally diverse, they will be remembered; there is no doubt about that.

There are two consequences of understanding the Orchid Effect. For the leader, it serves as an eye opener. Once he becomes aware of his limiting beliefs, he is more likely to focus on what is critical in the workplace, namely *work product* and *tangible output*. If superficial factors are outside societal norms, he may also help by giving this individual much needed input and feedback (using guidelines from the Diversity Foray).

For the culturally diverse person who is often equally unaware of the stereotyping that occurs, the Orchid Effect gives him a chance to manage the first four judgments. If he knows the rules of the game, it levels the playing field. Therefore, he is more likely to wear stylish clothes on his first day of work, for example, if his clothes sense typically falls short.

- We never get a second chance to make a first impression.
- At least this framework allows us to control a part of that first impression.

Author's note: Some of you may have an intense allergic reaction to this advice. Good. That means you are thinking for yourself and not just reading this book blindly. If you decide that you will be authentic to whatever your cultural norm is, I respect that. Obviously, I am assuming—as with all parts of the discussion—that this norm doesn't involve hurting others in any way and is within the limits of normal, moral behaviors. Never be afraid to wear that turban, bindi, burka, and so forth. Just be aware of how this will impact the five judgments.

Hopefully, as we continue on this journey, potential employers will look past the visually obvious cultural differences and will evaluate you based on your work product.

Another look at cultural stereotyping—the qualitative view:

So far we have analyzed the cost of cultural stereotyping in terms of more objective or measurable variables such as the delta (difference) between the work products of two similarly qualified candidates. But what about the qualitative costs of cultural stereotyping? *How do we quantify the loss of employee morale, good will, and discretionary energy at work?*

Diversity expertise comes from tackling both the art and science of the workplace dynamic.

Why do we care about cross cultural effectiveness in the workplace?

There are many reasons why this topic is important.

- First of all, *because it's the right thing to do.*
  - One shouldn't come to work feeling like one has to hide who one is, just because one comes from a different culture.
  - The learning from using cross cultural effectiveness techniques will help in dealing with other diversity aspects, such as age, gender, style, and educational background.

- Second, because it just makes so much business sense!
  - The amount of money, energy, and output that is wasted in a workplace because people are diminished and stressed out due to feeling *different* and ostracized is not trivial.
  - We live in a truly global world economy. We can no longer afford to be insular and stick to our little regional and national silos.

Let's illustrate this point with an example.

Real life example of the qualitative costs of cultural stereotyping:

(details adjusted for anonymity)

> A manager, Don, and his team were at a team celebration. One of the team members, Jim—an extraverted, personable man—was recounting a story about another team member, Eduardo, who was also present.
>
> He said, "Eduardo was saying . . . no, let me say that the way Eduardo would . . ." and then proceeded to tell the story imitating (in a very exaggerated manner) Eduardo's thick accent.
>
> The team laughed.
>
> The manager said nothing.
>
> Back at work, Eduardo was very quiet and withdrawn.

After a day or two, Eduardo went to his boss, Don, to explain how uncomfortable this encounter had been for him. (Kudos to Eduardo, by the way. In most cases, the wronged party does not mention it at all, for fear of negative consequences.)

Don, the manager, laughed it off and told Eduardo not to be so sensitive. It was "all in good fun" and meant nothing.

Eduardo reached out to friends and family for advice, which was very mixed. Not receiving any clear guidelines from his support system, Eduardo thought long and hard about what his next steps should be. He narrowed it down to the following options:

Report his manager Don and teammate Jim to Human Resources for an EEOC (Equal Employment Opportunity Commission) violation, since they had made him feel uncomfortable in the workplace. By the way, if one is physically out of the office but in a work-related team situation such as this, I believe that workplace norms of behavior are still expected.

Apply for *jobs in another company.*

Transfer to a *job in another function within the same company.*

Unfortunately, Eduardo was in the middle of his immigration process, whereby he was unable to legally change jobs—neither within the same company nor in a different organization.

Eduardo felt that it was dangerous to contact HR; he was dependent on Don for his immigration paperwork processing, which was critical for both him and his family.

So Eduardo waited it out for two years until he received his green card.

During that time, he spoke only when spoken to and was increasingly self-conscious about his thick accent. He was less productive than before—doing enough to get by but not volunteering for extra projects as he used to—and he was more present physically than mentally. The infectiously enthusiastic spirit, that had been his *distinguishing marker*, was markedly absent.

You may wonder why Eduardo had this extreme reaction to a seemingly trivial event.

Twist in the tale: Noticing Eduardo's unusual silence, Jim—the person who made the offensive comment—came to Eduardo and asked what was wrong. Eduardo explained and Jim apologized. This occurred a week after the incident.

That made little difference to Eduardo's negative state of mind, however. It was his boss Don who had let him down. That indeed was now the point of focus—that Eduardo reported to a boss who didn't value Eduardo's culture. Don had been perfectly happy to stand by while Eduardo was insulted and put down in public by a teammate.

It would be a great win if this book shows bosses like Don the *huge impact of seemingly trivial incidents on the career, productivity, and well-being of employees*.

Fortunately, this story ends on a positive note. After receiving his green card (two years later), Eduardo transferred to a new role within the same company, reporting thereafter to a more culturally adept and understanding boss. Under his new boss's tutelage, Eduardo blossomed into a highly valued, key contributor to the organization.

What lessons can we learn from Eduardo's example?

- If you are Eduardo?
- If you are Don, Eduardo's boss?
- If you are Eduardo's coworker, Jim, who made Eduardo feel so small?
- If you are another coworker of Eduardo's, who silently watched, tacitly giving Jim and Don permission to do nothing?

Victor Rivera, the debonair actor, activist, and author (*A Private Family Matter*) spoke eloquently during a national conference in Washington, DC on the dynamics behind domestic violence. One of the phenomena he referenced was extremely insightful and thought provoking:

During domestic violence incidents (which can start with mild bullying and then escalate), the *bully may test the waters to see how the public reacts*. So if a man slaps a woman, saying he is doing it "playfully," or pushes her roughly in a crowded bar, he then waits to see the reaction of bystanders.

If no one comes forward to say anything, the man may feel justified (by the implicit consent of the public's lack of a reaction) to continue, and even *escalate the violence in private.*

Take the phenomenon of bullying from a domestic to a workplace situation. The same logic applies. The more times we nip inappropriate cultural bullying in the bud, the less these issues escalate—and the less impact there is on productivity and the company's bottom line. *If you have a weak or unsympathetic boss like Don in a situation like this, coworkers have the right and the responsibility to stop the bullying cycle.*

We almost always have access to a really simple tool to break the cycle of workplace cross cultural bullying; it's the word *ouch*.

We don't have to put a lot of emotion in it—and we don't have to put ourselves in adversarial positions—just let Jim and Don know the stereotypical bullying is not appreciated, and has been noticed.

Ouch also conveys to Eduardo that at least one person on the team is not part of this conscious or unconscious put down. If those four powerful letters seem like too much of a risk, let's start smaller.

How about *not laughing* when a culturally offensive joke is shared in a group?

It's subtle, but better than implicit approval with your laughter.

Key Learning: *When diversity is used as a weapon to shame employees and leadership ignores this tactic, the entire business suffers.*

This book began with the phrase: *The journey of a thousand miles.* Each step we take, tiny or large, propels us forward on our foray, our journey, our movement.

You know how when you learn a new word you suddenly see it everywhere? If you read and truly assimilate this book's message, you will now notice how often people are made to feel small because they are different. And, in time, you will know how to reduce the frequency of this occurrence.

This is my hope and expectation for us all.

Key Learning: Section Three

- Reputational Currency, Physical Impact, Auditory Cues, Distinguishing Markers, and Work Product are the *Five Judgments of Stereotyping* in the workplace.
- The *Orchid Effect* is the composite of the five judgments and has powerful implications for workplace selection, promotion, and performance decisions.
- Part of the process leads to conscious and unconscious labels assigned to a person's organizational goodness of fit, hierarchical placement, and perceived danger level.
- There are qualitative and quantitative costs associated with our use of illogical stereotyping behaviors at work.
- If we empower and skill up people in our organization to be mature and adept at giving and receiving feedback, much of the negativity will seep out of the organization.
- We can reduce the cost of cultural stereotyping in the workplace by focusing more on the fifth judgment (work product) and being aware of our limiting beliefs around the more superficial visual, freshness, and auditory judgments.
- It is the joint responsibility of all to stop this cycle and show zero tolerance for blatant or subtle racial stereotyping.
- Authenticity is a critical factor in our behavioral choices.

Section Four

Cultural Norms: a Practical Global Toolkit

Rules of engagement, workplace norms, and
effective multi cultural techniques.

To find out what one is fitted to do, and to secure an opportunity to do it, is the key to happiness.

John Dewey

Chapter 17

Unwritten Rules of Engagement

Are you reading your organization's culture cues?

I was fortunate enough to visit the new Facebook headquarters in California last year. In the huge hallways where there are hundreds of workstations, each employee gets to hang a flag of his native country above his cube in the communal workspace. So as you walk along the aisles, you can see from a distance which person is from Brazil, Switzerland, or Nigeria.

What a powerful organizational cue: this is a place that values cultural diversity!

Look around your organization using a diversity lens.

Ask yourself:

- Are there functioning diversity groups or initiatives?
- Are these groups culturally diverse on multiple fronts, or do they focus only on one aspect of race or culture?
- Does the diversity director only see things as black versus white, or shades of brown and gray? Does he

take into account other factors of diversity, such as gender and style?

- Are there any Hispanics or women of color on the leadership team?
- Which cultural or religious holidays are celebrated officially by the organization?

The organization's cultural cues are all around you; you just have to know what to look for.

A manager I respect deeply (for his political savvy, among other things,) has a basic hypothesis that has resonated with me over the years. His premise is that each person has a *normal distribution* of behavioral range. Once you know what that range and average is, you can assess whether someone's behavior is typical or not, based on this baseline.

For example, if your boss is always direct to the point of rudeness, you normalize your expectations according to the way he usually behaves. So if he sends you a one-word email response—"No"—you don't take it personally. It is part of his persona.

On the other hand, if he starts being overly effusive with someone, you take note. What's going on here? Did he just hear he's going to be laid off? Has HR spoken to him about being so blunt? Normalize a person based on their typical behavioral range.

Taking this concept one step further, we can *normalize the organization* as a whole on certain key variables, including cultural diversity. Typically, organizational culture assessments *gauge which behaviors and standard operating processes* make businesses more profitable and which reduce productivity due to reduced morale or inefficient practices.

If we want to develop an organization's cultural diversity skills, first we must assess where the organization stands on these aspects.

First, we develop a baseline snapshot of the current situation, using multiple question surveys. These are either online or interview style, maintaining complete confidentiality. We therefore uncover messaging around dress code, decision-making processes, speed of execution, and subtler employee engagement and protocol related anecdotal evidence.

Next, we decide which elements should remain and are working for the company's profitability. Finally, we target a few key, undesirable elements of the organization's culture for change.

What does one get rewarded for in this company?

- Hard work versus output
- Reactive firefighting versus proactive planning skills
- Being pleasant and flattering the boss, not rocking the boat

What will get you in trouble at work?

- Working overly long hours or low output
- Being direct or not being direct (when there are differing points of view)

Illustrative example of assessing, and responding to, organizational cues:

When Leonardo moved from a managerial role in a midsized company to an executive role in a Fortune 500 company, his politically savvy friend and former colleague, Julia, gave him great advice. Recognizing the difference between the two organizations' cultures, Julia cautioned Leonardo about managing his initial brand or buzz.

Leonardo's development budget in his earlier role had been a fraction of his current budget. Further, no expense was spared in the new organization when holding training events. Expensive leather binders and name brand apparel was purchased for workshop participants; high-end consultant fees and five-star hotel dinners were *de rigueur*.

Julia's exact words to Leonardo were: "Make sure you don't get a reputation for being cheap. You are moving in a different league now." That was great advice, from someone who cared enough to be straightforward with him. What Julia didn't add (but which both were aware of, reading between the lines) was: "especially since you are from a different culture." This ties in to reputational currency in the Five Judgments. To summarize, read your organizational cues—which are all around you.

Does being different work *for* you, or *against* you?

While Distinguishing Markers hold some of the answers to this question, the other critical components are organizational culture and interpersonal fit. Even within different functions of the same organization, powerful subcultures coexist. For example, the Ops (operations) department may function in a diametrically opposite manner compared to the same company's marketing group.

There is also a *timing awareness* skill in managing our differentiators positively or negatively.

When you act—and what you say and do—can be as important as **how** you behave.

In interviews and conversations with successful minority representatives (whether the variable of diversity was ethnicity, generation, or gender) a pattern emerged for many respondents. They used a surprisingly consistent, and effective strategy, which was powerful because of the sequence of events. In other words, step one was followed by step two, which was followed by step three.

Unleashing the Power of Diversity Process Flow (step by step sequence):

1. Observe the behavior.
2. Analyze normative and punitive organizational messages.
3. Fit in *unless doing so compromises your critical values*.
4. Build group trust with high quality deliverables, character, and work ethic.
5. Allow your natural uniqueness to show; notice if differentiators are appreciated or viewed with trepidation.
6. If you care and dare enough, *unleash your power of diversity with well thought out acts of courage that move the organization forward*.

In other words, the general recommendation is to use your eyes and ears first. Analyze team and organizational practices, see what behaviors are exhibited by thought leaders, and observe the unspoken norms of the group. Deliver great products, be on time and reliable, and develop your reputational currency that you are a valuable, trustworthy addition to the team.

Then start adding your unique flavor to the mix. Do so with courage and integrity, until you find your strength, your voice; this is known as *unleashing the power of diversity*.

The benefits of using this step-by-step process are that *you alienate fewer people at the point of initial contact*. Going in with guns blazing may be ineffective for new team members or leaders. Obviously there is an element of common sense in this advice; self-awareness and political savvy must come into play. There will be some rules that you are very comfortable with, while others will be different from your set of unwritten rules.

This allows you to decide, in the interest of authenticity, which of the opposing rules is worth fighting for. That line is drawn in the sand in different places for each person. You may draw the line in terms of protecting your name because it's important to you. When you walk into a room where you are the only representative of your culture, someone will change your name from Alessandro to Alex.

Do you choose to draw attention to yourself *because holding onto your original name is very important to you?* I am the same way, firmly holding on to this essential piece of my identity regardless of the costs involved. However, if interacting for the first time with a potential client who calls me "Deb" after I have corrected him once, it appears practical to let it go.

Many culturally diverse professionals permanently shorten their names to sound more western because this is a fight they don't want to take on day after day. Are they right? Am I right? There is no valid right answer. These are personal choices we all make in day-to-day living.

The bottom line is that if you are different, *know the unwritten rules* before making choices about whether to stand out or to conform. Then make a conscious decision as to which rules you are comfortable following,

While unwritten rules can be organization specific, country specific, and leader specific, after multiple conversations, here are the ten most important factors that can impact your presence at work:

Top Ten Unwritten Norms in a Western Business Environment:

- ➢ A professional and well groomed physical presence
- ➢ Crisp verbal and written communication skills
- ➢ Political savvy and awareness of organizational power players
- ➢ A focus on individual accomplishments and reward
- ➢ Punctuality with deadlines and meetings
- ➢ An appropriate lack of deference (or fear) toward management at senior levels
- ➢ A sense of humor
- ➢ Being easy to talk to, never defensive
- ➢ Familiarity with local culture (including sports, music, television, and movies)
- ➢ A well packaged and presented work product

Top 10 Unwritten Norms in an Eastern Business Environment:

> ➤ Respect for one's manager using verbal and nonverbal messaging
> ➤ Understanding and following hierarchical protocol (table seating assumed by rank, for example)
> ➤ Respect toward books and learning-related objects
> ➤ Accepting invitations for evening or social events
> ➤ Hospitality toward overseas visitors outside business hours
> ➤ Not asking difficult questions in a group meeting; if important, asking them one on one
> ➤ Impressing others with volume and speed (both aspects: speaking loudly, fast, and saying a lot)
> ➤ Effusive body language: head nods, bowing while reading business cards, hand gestures.
> ➤ Dressing modestly and appropriately.*
> ➤ Focus and praise for the team, not the individual

*Dressing modestly and appropriately usually means women in high-necked tops with slacks rather than skirts, and men in suits or dress pants, not jeans and T-shirts.

It may be useful to reflect on the implicit rules in your specific organization.

Top 10 Unwritten Norms in my workplace:

➢ Respect for (years of experience, technical expertise)
_____

➢ Trust (for senior leaders, for my team, is low/high)
_____

➢ Decision making processes are (hierarchical, egalitarian)
_____

➢ Honesty or indirectness (is there backbiting when a person leaves the room?) _____

➢ People are promoted for (hard work or output?)
_____

➢ Successful people here are (extraverts, go getters, political, honest) _____

➢ Written communication (information overload or need to know basis?) _____

➢ Dress code _____

➢ Reward and recognition for (team or individual?)
_____

➢ Other _____

Are your unwritten rules the same as your boss'?
     Yes_____ No_____

Where do they differ? _____

Your organization's leader? Yes_____ No_____

Where do they differ? _____

Your direct reports (if applicable)? Yes_____ No_____

Where do they differ? _____

When entering a new work environment, whether Western or Eastern, these key pointers will serve as a baseline in various situations: a *how to* list. Obviously, your success in applying this list will depend on the country you are coming from or going to, your command over the native language, and so on. Nonetheless, these lists of unwritten norms will help you develop your own customized list.

Some other techniques that work well are:

> ➤ Acquiring a mentor or *culture teacher*
> ➤ Watching how successful people from similar backgrounds navigate unknown territories
> ➤ Continuous improvement and being open to feedback
> ➤ Making assumptions of positive intent when people give you difficult, constructive feedback
> ➤ Paying it forward when you have integrated successfully into the local environment

So far, we have focused on two key target groups for this book:

First, the **mainstream leader** who, by improving interactions at work with diverse colleagues, direct reports, clients or geographies, **increases business performance**.

Second, the **diverse employee,** who benefits professionally and personally by **learning how to thrive in new environments.**

For the rest of this section, we explore both tactical and strategic elements of our practical global toolkit, such as dress code, communication norms, ways to build reputational currency and trust, and a special focus on powerful questioning techniques.

Chapter 18

Dress Code

Let's assume that you are offered the job you wanted after following the pointers, using your natural skills, and completing an excellent interview. The organization makes you a generous offer, which you promptly accept. Not only did you earn reputational currency, but also you made strategic use of the five judgments to create a good impression during your interview.

Now you are getting ready for your first day at work, where you get to meet with your boss again and with your coworkers for the first time. Remember, a question from the first section of the book: Is cross cultural effectiveness about being different? Or fitting in?

The road to success lies in the following two ways:

First, find out the unwritten norms and rules of appearance and behavior. Where it doesn't clash strongly with your culture, try to blend in first. Let your difference of clothing and dress not be what distracts people from seeing you as a person. Once your boss and colleagues recognize you as a person, start bringing more of yourself into work. I would give the same advice to women in a male-dominated workplace or to millennials entering baby boomer strongholds. *Do not let something superficial like attire give people a negative first impression of you.*

- That being said, once you have chosen your outfit, wear it with pride.
- Own the room with confidence and *gravitas.*
- Remind yourself that you *never* get a second chance to make a first impression.

Example based on real life events:

You are invited to your first office Christmas party. You dress really well, in expensive stylish clothes. Unfortunately, when you reach the well-decorated foyer of the country club where the reception is being held, you are dismayed to find that you are the only one wearing purple. Eighty percent of the guests are wearing red or green, with a few black dresses scattered around the room.

If it is too late to do anything about it, make a mental note so you don't repeat the issue next year, and try very hard to forget it. Chances are that it will mean less to others than it does to you. Let it go.

Author's note: Obviously if you have to dress a certain way for religious or other reasons, these guidelines won't apply. If you are Farida, a Muslim female who wears a burka to work, you may take the advice about shoes, but ignore other pointers, obviously.

Let's start from the floor and move up.

Shoes

Men:

- Comfortable black or dark brown leather shoes.
- No white socks and dark shoes *(Sorry, David Letterman)*.
- No white shoes and dark socks with dress pants, either.
- No sandals at work.
  - Unless you get a job at IDEO, or hear for certain that this is your organization's norm, trust me on this one.

Women:

- Leather shoes, comfortable, closed toes, two-inch heel.
- No flats or wobbly four-inch stiletto heels.

Author's note: Is this prescriptive? Certainly! When you have worked for awhile, you can wear beautiful black and white stiletto heels. They call me Imelda (after the infamous Ms. Marcos) due to the ridiculous number of shoes I possess. So I certainly don't wear closed two-inch heel basic shoes these days. But you'll have fewer chances of going wrong in safe and conservative footwear initially.

Accessories

Men:

- Black or brown leather attaché or laptop bag.
- Leather belts, medium wide, in good condition.

- Avoid digital sports watches or ones with alarm clock style faces.
- Cuff links are no longer considered fashionable.
- *A reputable midrange watch like a Movado* is preferable to a fake Rolex.
- Strong overpowering cologne detracts from your brand.

Women:

- Black or brown leather purse or laptop bag.
- Avoid pearls unless you have specific information otherwise.
  - A single strand of matched pearls is considered old fashioned in many organizations (unless the beads are asymmetric or bunched in clusters).

- One or two classy pieces of jewelry (real or costume) is a happy medium.
  - A good rule is: put on jewelry, and then take off one piece.
  - Gold-accented jewelry with a brown outfit is fine for the more mature.
  - Silver jewelry with black or navy works across the board.

Yes, I know that beautiful, purple slouch bags are in vogue. But a good rule of thumb is to go for a timeless classic look that will still be considered stylish five years from now. We are going for a *brand* here. If you take care of expensive, timeless accessories—given the cyclicality of fashion trends—you may be able to use these classic pieces for decades.

Apparel (clothing)

Men:

- Slacks or jeans?
  - ○ Find out the company norm.
  - ○ Dress pants or slacks are usually safe.
- Shirt or golf shirt?
  - ○ It's hard to go wrong with a good quality dress shirt.
  - ○ In some organizations a golf shirt with collar is acceptable.

Women:

- Pants or skirts?
  - ○ In most western workplaces, you are safer coming to work in trousers the first day.
  - ○ Absolutely no midriff showing with short tops. Nonnegotiable.
- A basic shell with a soft jacket or long sleeved shirt on top is professional and understated.
- Avoid ruffles and flowery prints.
- A splash of some color is acceptable (burnt amber, teal, or ombré leaf: look it up!). Avoid pink, red, and yellow.

Overall guidelines:

- Hair is very critical; it should be stylish but not outrageous.
- Nothing you wear should be torn, worn, or frayed looking.
- Make sure your clothes have no sweat marks.

- We have already discussed how critical the absence of body odor is.
- The **trick is not looking like you tried too hard.** Middle of the road (width, color, designs).
- The brand you are going for (both genders) is stylish, confident, assured, and polished.
- Pants should fit well. *Both genders: we don't need to see muffin tops or beer bellies.*
- The small investment you make to buy the necessary items will be returned twofold in brand building.
- Start building your professional presence when you walk in that door.
- Women, this is especially critical. Be cognizant of your presence. Does your physical impact proclaim I'm a sweet girly girl?

It's quite possible you will read all this and just dress the way you always have. That's fine. I just want to make sure you don't show up at work without making some conscious choices. Whether they are yours or mine is of no consequence.

To summarize, regarding your physical presence:

➤ Be a detective: observe your peers and uncover implicit organizational dress codes.
➤ Match the norm initially, if financially feasible.
➤ Remember and manage the five judgments.
➤ Aim for a stylish appearance overall that exudes freshness and good grooming.

Chapter 19

Communication Guidelines

> *"I would appreciate recommendations for contractors who put down marbles in the bathroom . . ."*
>
> (This is a real quote, a sincere and innocent request for a marble flooring contractor referral.)

If you are not sure what the joke is in the "I would appreciate . . ." sentence above, please ask someone who is a native or fluent English speaker to explain it to you. The point being: **Do you know what to say, regardless of the situation, and how to say it?**

Communication is that which is understood.

The most basic purpose of communication is to understand, and maybe more importantly, to be understood. Each of us has our own communication style. Part of it is our natural style and some of it is what we see growing up (which has a huge cultural component). The rest relates to positive and negative messaging reinforcement that we have received throughout our lives.

The first step is to have a basic knowledge of the workplace language. It's like Maslow's hierarchy of needs: it would be shortsighted to expect a starving person to strive toward self-actualization when his stomach is empty. Someone who cannot understand basic English conversations should start by attending English proficiency classes. The rest of this chapter assumes that you have a good working grasp of the language.

So, the key questions in cross cultural communication are:

- What is my communication style and overall brand?
- What is the communication norm associated with this organization's culture?
- What is my specific message?
- What are my options for sending it?
- How is it being sent?
- How is it being received?
- Do I need to tweak my message, process, or medium?

Scenario:

You are working in England. You suddenly learn that your sister, who lives in Japan, is seriously ill. You would like to leave work immediately to go and look after her for a few weeks.

Your first instinct might be to just dive into the message and say:

"I have to go to Japan tomorrow and spend three weeks there to look after my sick sister."

If, instead, you ask a series of questions to analyze the situation and your options, you will become a more powerful influencer. We are more likely to get our desired short-term outcomes, as well as maintain our long-term relationship with our boss, if we are strategic and skillful communicators.

- Your communication brand; ask yourself the following questions:
  - Does my boss grant me most of my requests?
  - Do I use this privilege sparingly?
  - Am I high maintenance, always trying to squeeze every last drop of blood from a stone?
  - Or am I relatively easy going and laid back?
  - Have I pitched in when someone else on the team had a family emergency?
- The organization's cultural norm:
  - Does this Oxford based organization value family ties?
  - Does my boss take a lot of time off for personal issues?

- In Japan, a sick sister is very important. Is that true in this office in the UK?
- The specific message:
  - What exactly am I asking for?
    - Three weeks totally off the grid, or with a wireless card and cell phone?
  - Will I be able to meet most of my deadlines?
  - When I come back, am I planning to catch up on those deadlines?
  - Would I like my boss to assign some critical tasks to my coworkers?
- Options and choices:
  - Am I high performing?
  - Am I in a position of strength or weakness?
  - If in a *two strikes zone,* will I jeopardize my job? If so, should I be very tactful and offer multiple options?
- How is the request being signaled?
  - Am I demanding or cajoling?
  - Is this so important that this is nonnegotiable, or am I willing to compromise to meet the organization's needs?
- How is the message being received?
- What is my boss's body language?
  - Supportive, guilty, angry, stressed out?
- Tweaking the message process and medium:
  - What power can I exert in this moment, to mirror back some of the emotions and manage this diversity between us?
  - Should I have given my boss a phone heads up versus just walking over to his office and asking?
  - Is my boss an introvert who needs to reflect before making a decision?

As always, let's go back and test our process using the Diversity Foray:

* Ask * Adapt * Accept * Appreciate

> ➢ Did I use the guidelines correctly when *asking* for the favor?
> ➢ Am I *adapting* to the situation and workplace needs?
> ➢ Can I *accept* a refusal if it comes?
> ➢ Do I *appreciate* how my boss (in spite of coming from a culture where one doesn't leave work to help sisters) is trying to accommodate me?

Don't *SPACE* out! Particularly don't *assume* or *escalate*.

Applying Communication Norms to Business Situations

A multi cultural communication example: bluntness versus politically correct speech

Many years ago, I had the privilege of interacting with and collecting data from some delightful Japanese colleagues and visitors. The group was mixed; some had just landed in the United States directly from Japan, and others had been in North America for several years. Those who had just landed in the United States had fascinating insights. It took awhile to get their candid impressions (because they were naturally courteous and indirect).

After patient and nonthreatening forms of questioning, here were some of their perceptions about American culture:

Example 1: Kaga San arrives in Houston, Texas directly from Japan and remarks:

"Couples in the US say 'Honey, I love you, love you, sweetheart' every day, yet the divorce rate is over 50 percent?"

"Everything is *big* here: ice cream, buildings, hair . . . and people!"

Example 2: Texans travel from Houston to Tokyo to close a critical deal:

A group of Western negotiators travel to Japan to settle a high level deal. Elated, they call the head office with excellent news. The discussions have gone great; they are close to sealing the deal.

When they go to sign the papers the next week, they are surprised to find that the meeting has been cancelled, the Japanese leader is "busy," and eventually the deal falls through.

What happened?

There was a communication and styles misunderstanding. In a clash of styles (highly indirect versus blunt and to the point), the key messages short circuited.

At the initial meeting, when the (assertive, fast talking, charming) western negotiator proposed terms, his Japanese counterpart said "Ah, so interesting." That's the kiss of death. Typically, in a negotiation of this nature, that could mean (if you were reading the body language correctly) not just *no*, but *hell, no!*

Not picking up on the cues, the more excited and pushy the negotiator became, the more the Japanese group retired, eventually hiding behind a wall of unavailability.

The lesson from this anecdote is about doing your homework. Have someone with you from Japan (particularly for critical multimillion yen deals), or an expert who understands the subtle sighs and use of phrases.

People speak, e-mail, and write a certain way because of deeply entrenched beliefs about what constitutes poor or effective communication.

This is a key factor for when we give culturally diverse people feedback.

Does the person we are leading, coaching, or mentoring have a firmly held belief, or definitions of effective and ineffective output for this area (communication in this case)? Is it the same as ours?

The United States can be a source of mystery to people from other countries as far as directness of style goes. A high percentage of compliments, sometimes even bordering on insincerity, is often associated with American social communication styles.

And yet, the *brand* for US business interactions is *candid and direct* to the extreme. There are senior leaders who will respond with one word: *Yes,* or *No,* to a two-page e-mail from a division in Asia. They will "tell it like it is" when a supplier misses a deadline, and they generally pride themselves on their bluntness and honesty.

And then, the same man who was brutally honest at work will go back home to a corpulent spouse, and tell her how great she looks in an unflattering outfit—and do so with a straight face. It's part of a culture where a casual acquaintance will say, "Did you cut your hair? I **love** it!" or "That color really suits you," for example. This is one paradox that—according to multiple informal interviews—puzzles people from Europe (especially the UK, Germany, and Russia!) and Asia in general. This is because the accepted communication norms for bluntness versus kindness vary greatly by region.

Thus, a genuine compliment may be mistaken as lip service. When the same person says the same positive thing to five people, the compliment loses its value.

If compliments are a dime a dozen, it's an all-you-can-eat buffet. After a while you don't feel like going back for thirds or fourths, and it's not as appealing. But if you have a seafood dinner every now and then, the special meal has more value because it occurs rarely and was achieved at some cost. This characteristic (too much effusiveness as a society) is part of the brand of the United States. It sounds harsh, but my role here is to share perceptions across the board.

On the flip side, the United States communication style is usually very pleasant, and the warmth makes people feel good about themselves.

So what's the negative communication style brand for people from Asia? Certain countries are known for being honest and blunt; however, this pendulum may have swung to the other extreme. Too much honesty—to the point of hurtfulness—can be used as a weapon under the guise of *it's for your own good*.

Keep in mind that Japan is technically within Asia, so once again, it's very risky to generalize. If I say South Americans are very passionate and loud in their communication styles, is that equally true about Venezuelans as it is about Colombians? So also, Australia and Europe have completely divergent interaction styles, depending on the country.

It is dangerous to climb the slippery slope of generalization.

The main purpose of this section was to reflect on our personal communication style and our country's perceived communication style. This was the objective of the self-assessment in Section One. As you gain self-awareness, go back to this question in a few months, and see if your answers change.

Chapter 20

Feedback skills

In this section, we will briefly focus on giving and receiving feedback more effectively.

When I was studying chemical engineering, we used feedback in a different context.

Basically, feedback is the process by which information about what has occurred can change the outcome of what will occur. Because this forms a kind of loop, the action is said to *feed back* (into itself).

Feedback has been defined in engineering terms as "information about the gap between the actual level and the reference level of a system parameter, which is used to alter the gap in some way," emphasizing that the information itself is not feedback unless translated into action.

Let's think about this for a minute. Feedback in the business world would benefit from following these guidelines as well, in my opinion.

- What is the point of giving and receiving feedback if no action results from it?

- For positive feedback, the resulting action is that the person should continue, or even increase, the same behavior.
- For negative feedback, the resulting action would be for the person to correct his course if possible.
- Feedback that just sits there—with the intention of making the giver powerful or putting down the receiver—is just a waste of airtime.

If you reject someone's feedback, the action should be twofold. First, tuck away the information as your first data point. If a week (or a month, or a year) later someone else gives you similar input, you should take notice, as it's the second occurrence. A third occurrence validates the original feedback, as the data has now moved from a single point to a line and has become a pattern.

In the transaction of giving feedback, clearly there are at least two parties involved: the feedback **giver** and **receiver**. Let's examine the responsibilities of both roles.

How to give feedback effectively:

Make sure there is an *ask* as well as a *tell* when giving feedback, particularly in cross cultural situations. Talk about what is or isn't working as soon as possible after the event occurs, for maximum impact. Allow for the possibility of there being more than one right answer, or there being extenuating circumstances. Stay focused on the subject at hand; don't allow red herrings to distract you.

> *The editors of this book personified the art of giving feedback with care and directness.* Thanks to their invaluable suggestions, this book is more readable. Effective questioning styles can be coupled with giving feedback so there is both an *ask* and a *tell*. For example, a particular cultural example appeared four times in the first draft. By asking why this diversity space was particularly important to me personally, my editors helped me craft a better book and increase my self-awareness.

Giving valuable feedback skillfully is both an art and a science. If you are fortunate enough to come across a feedback maestro, watch him carefully. You will learn a lot by osmosis.

How to give effective feedback in difficult workplace situations:

If a person talks too much at meetings (in your opinion), one way you could address the issue would be to say "Bobby, you spoke too much at this morning's meeting." Crude, but honest.

Perhaps a better way would be to check in as to how self-aware Bobby is. "How do you think the meeting went this morning, Bobby?" Bobby may respond, "I thought it was great" or "I was so nervous, I couldn't stop talking." So asking first to assess the recipient's self-awareness is time well spent.

Next, be direct without damaging the relationship. Choose the location and situation carefully. Make sure you have enough time for both of you to say what needs to be said. Of course, use the normal feedback protocol; address the issue, not the person. Add any cultural context you can.

For example, you may effectively give Bobby the feedback message as follows:

"Bobby, there were ten people at today's staff meeting. Typically *airtime*, or time each person speaks, is divided evenly, so each person would speak about 10 percent of the time. It looked to me like you spoke for about 25 percent of the time. Do you agree with my assessment?"

Bobby can then respond one of three ways.

- Bobby may become really defensive and say he spoke more because the topic was in his area of expertise.

- Bobby may be genuinely surprised, open to the feedback but saying nothing as he thoughtfully considers this new information.
- Bobby could absorb the feedback, thank you for giving it, and ask for suggestions to address this issue moving forward.

Let's reconnect with reality. The third, ideal option rarely happens at the outset. However, as we build our feedback muscles, we usually attain the desired behavior change over time.

Assuming that Bobby and you (the feedback giver in this example) have a reasonably high trust relationship, you would, perhaps in the next conversation, move into the reason you gave him the feedback—for instance, the negative impact that his high use of airtime can have on his career and success. You might point out the link between speaking—either too much or too little—and Bobby's personal presence and brand. That this could be a career-limiting factor. It would depend on Bobby's emotional maturity, as well as your mutual trust. Also, remember that Bobby may have reached his current level of success by being super aggressive in a highly competitive, hostile environment. So be prepared to show him how to adapt to the new norms of desirable behavior.

Let's bring back our Diversity Foray as a safety net for giving feedback.

Do *ask, adapt, accept, and appreciate* as appropriate.

The issue is bounded by two parameters: the disconnect between Bobby's current behavior (and the organizational norm) and the overall goal of improving Bobby's brand, and thereby his long-term success.

How to receive feedback effectively

For years, trainers and consultants have taught us "There *is only one response to receiving negative feedback,* and that is . . . ?" And we, in the audience, would respond "Thank you."

This is no longer my position on receiving feedback, particularly in the context of cross cultural feedback. All too often, we end up coaching people who leave a trail of damage from their inaccurate and hurtful feedback. Biased stereotypical perceptions of cultural groups can make cross cultural feedback not just untrue, but downright harmful. Therefore, my amended advice to you would be "In *most situations,* receive feedback for improvement by saying thank you."

When you believe that feedback is being used as a weapon of attack:

- Get other people, or data, to validate or refute the inputs.
- Be careful you don't pick someone overly positive toward you, to fool yourself that the feedback was harsh.
- If the data is not valid, decide how much energy you want to spend on arguing with the feedback giver.
- A great tool is to say: "I believe you meant well when you gave me this feedback." You can add a thank you or not, depending on the situation.
- You don't have to agree with something to listen to it. Clarify that as well. "X, just to clarify, I am nodding to show I am listening. It doesn't mean either agreement or disagreement with your opinion."

- And of course, the good old fall back: "Let's agree to disagree."

Sometimes the feedback is both accurate *and* being used to draw blood. What then? My recommendation is to try to keep control over your expressions. Think *poker face*. Agree to some of the valid points, but don't say a lot more. Apologize if needed, but do so appropriately.

Being cocky and closed to feedback causes the individual to stop growing in every aspect of life.

Being obsequious and apologizing for every little issue is ineffective as well.

Somewhere in between lies the sweet spot, where you are appropriately humble and open to learning, yet you retain your dignity and respect.

Being different in and of itself is nothing to be ashamed about.

Chapter 21

Building Trust

So much about building trust has to do with cross cultural communication. Knowing what to say and how to say it increases mutual trust and respect. There is also a strong correlation between building trust and reputational currency. There are several well known Trust Frameworks. The Reina Trust Model, in my opinion, is an excellent guide toward understanding and leveraging trust.

The Reina Trust and Betrayal Model

According to the Reina model, there are three major types of trust:

- *Contractual* (to do with your character: do you manage expectations and boundaries well, keep agreements, how consistent are you?)
- *Competence* (to do with capability: do you trust that others are good at what they do and let them learn and ask questions?)
- *Communication* (to do with disclosure, truthfulness, and admitting to mistakes)

It is important to make these distinctions because there are multiple aspects to trust building.

How to build trust and reputational currency:

1. Be relentlessly good at what you do.
2. Make a connection, not a sale.
3. Find time to network, even when you think you don't have time to network.
4. Remember, the people you kicked on your way up are the people who will be waiting with javelins on your way down.
5. Help people who need it, regardless of whether you see any short-term benefits or not.
6. Receive feedback openly.
7. Remain true to *you*, your authentic style, your mission, and your culture.
8. Let things go.
9. Develop a name for strength with kindness.
10. Be appropriately flexible.

1. *Be relentlessly good at what you do.*
   If you aren't good at what you do, either find something that is more of a match for you, or get better at your current vocation.

2. *Make a connection, not a sale.*
   The best person I know for this skill set is a consultant I worked with who never asked for business. He always remembered who likes to ski in Aspen, who has five dogs, and which baseball team an EVP was passionate about. And it wasn't forced or phony. I cannot emphasize how critical social connections are.

3. *Find time to network, even when you think you don't have time to network.*
   By the time we reach a certain age, we can spot BS a mile away. Don't you hate it when people who didn't care at all about you suddenly reach out to you because they want something? People are not stupid.

4. *Remember, the people you kicked on your way up are the people who will be waiting with javelins on your way down.* Need I say more? If you only knew how many times I have personally experienced this. People tend to manage up better than they manage laterally or down. The body bags you leave along the way will come back to haunt you.

5. *Help people who need it, regardless of whether you see any short-term benefits or not.*
   It befits us to be especially kind to people who have been laid off or are looking for work. Obviously that's the right thing to do, but the added practical bonus is that people really remember who helped them when they were struggling . . . and which rats left a sinking ship in a hurry.

6. *Receive feedback openly.*
   Don't be defensive; accept that to the person giving the feedback, this impression is the truth. Be aware that in cross cultural effectiveness, context is critical and may override general feedback rules. Before you change anything, assess if this feedback is skewed because of the giver's cultural biases.

7. *Remain true to you, your authentic style, your mission, and your culture.*
   Clarity on your mission defines your aura, your presence. So often people fake behaviors, accents, and mannerisms in order to fit in. It's not even about "you can fool some of the people some of the time, but not all of the people all of the time." It's more about the intense productivity surges that people feel when their real voice is heard and understood—not necessarily agreed with, just heard and understood.

8. *Let things go.*
   You may have been holding on to a dream in which life is perfect. Let it go. You may expect to live in a perfect world, where everything is fair and just. Let it go. You may be subjected to petty behavior from small minded people. Let it go. There is a beautiful saying that goes, "I wish you enough." Study after study shows that people who have a positive outlook on life tend to develop more resilience and experience more happiness. Life is a package deal. Holding onto grudges or unrealistic expectations cripples our chances of being the best at what we are, or can be.

9. *Develop a name for honesty with kindness.*
   Time and again people hurt each other's feelings in the guise of being honest. They may get a cheap thrill by

drawing blood and it's not about honesty at all. Kindness means being completely blunt when needed, to stop someone you care about from falling face down. At the same time, kindness means you don't make a person feel small, particularly in front of others.

10. *Be appropriately flexible.*

Have you noticed that there are always certain people you avoid at work? Some of them are actually very skilled. But, because they are demanding and inflexible, we avoid them. Make sure you are not one of those people whom others avoid. Being easy to work with (without being a pushover) is a skill. People who respond well in a crunch develop a great brand; asking "how high?" every time a leader says "jump" destroys your buzz. That's why the *appropriately flexible* combination is needed.

Key Learning: Section Four

- Cross cultural effectiveness has significant business impact in a global economy.

- At times being different works for us; other times being different works against us.

- Leaders can increase morale and reduce attrition by displaying savvy diversity behaviors.

- When we embrace diversity and promote inclusion, we truly *unleash the power of diversity*.

- There is a different set of unwritten norms for employees in Western and Eastern cultures.

- Learn the unwritten norms for success in your organization and analyze whether you are fitting in, standing out in a negative way, or perceived as being valuably unique.

- Giving and receiving feedback effectively is a key skill to bridge diversity gaps.

- Be open to receiving feedback, while weighing the intent and validity of the feedback.

- Trust and reputational currency are built slowly, by following some key guidelines.

- Managing one's reputational currency is worth the effort for one's personal and professional growth.

Section Five

Conclusion

"If you have no faith in yourself, then have faith in the things you call truth.
You know what must be done.
You may not have courage or trust or understanding or the will to do it,
but you know what must be done.
You can't turn back.
There is no answer behind you.
You fear what you cannot name.
So look at it and find a name for it.
Turn your face forward and learn.
Do what must be done."

Patricia A. McKillip

Chapter 22

Call to Action

> *People speak to us in two languages: the language of words and the language of emotions. Make sure you listen for them both.*

Our diversity journey starts and ends with empathy.

Not with blind agreement, but with being able to see things from another's perspective.

Henry Ford once said:

"If there is any great secret of success in life, it lies in the ability to put yourself in the other person's place and to see things from his point of view—as well as your own."

In the diversity world, we call this the Platinum Rule.

Remember the Golden Rule?

Do unto others as you would have them do unto *you*?

The Platinum Rule works even better:

Do unto others as you would have them do unto themselves.

But in order to do that, you have to understand them first. Several years ago, a realization dawned on me:

> *People talk to us in two languages: the language of words and the language of emotions. Make sure you listen to them both. If you aren't able to read the second language, observe the attendant actions and a pattern will emerge.*

It is my sincere hope that this book has helped you in this quest for understanding.

And, more importantly, I hope it will propel you to action by arming you with a practical new global toolkit.

> *So what now?*
>
> *So what?*
>
> *So now what?*

We started our journey together in a bustling internet café in the Americas. As we come full circle, it is fitting that the Grande Cappuccino has morphed into pure Darjeeling tea, sipped in the tranquility of a beautiful trellised verandah (patio) in Asia.

Butterflies hover over alabaster anthurrium.

I take a deep breath and reflect on the topic of multi cultural competence.

And it strikes me that *competence* in this area is no longer enough.

As Cecil Beaton says: "Be daring, be different, be impractical, be anything that will assert integrity of purpose and imaginative vision against the play-it-safers, the creatures of the commonplace, the slaves of the ordinary".

With every act of gracefulness and gratefulness, every diversity interaction well executed for business results, my challenge to you is that we set the bar even higher.

Where being "creatures of the commonplace" is no longer an option.

When we stop playing it safe and truly unleash our diverse talent, who knows what greatness we can collectively aspire to?

> I see you.
>
> You are as me, caught in what Covey called 'the thick of thin things".
>
> Take a deep breath, as I did a moment ago.
>
> You read this book because diversity meant something to you, at the very core of your being.
>
> It is no longer a question of whether you can afford to unleash this power.
>
> It is a question of whether you can afford *not to.*

I reach out this baton of change to you across the continents. Do you take it eagerly, arms outstretched?

There is *no moment in time but this one*, fleeting and ephemeral; powerful in its fragility.

Together, *shall we seize this moment?*

And, *gathering momentum, make it momentous?*

All movements start with a single, small step.

What will yours be?

Debjani Mukherjee Biswas
USA India Planet Earth

Appendix

Action Planning Worksheet

The next few pages have an action planning work sheet, followed by charts on key aspects of cultural diversity: religious groups, populations, and languages.

Please take a few minutes to commit to at least one specific action you will take as a result of reading this book.

It could be as simple as using the *Astute *Strong *Kind approach to asking tough diversity questions, or it could be establishing a long-term diversity strategy for your company, which includes Five Judgments awareness training in all interviewing situations.

The expectation is that there will be at least one action to justify the time taken reading this book and absorbing these new concepts.

One concept I learned from this book that really resonated with me was:

_____
_____
_____

It will be useful for me at work and/or at home because:

_____
_____
_____

The specific action I plan to take based on what I read in *Unleash the Power of Diversity* is:

_____

_____

_____

I plan to complete this task by _____
(insert date here).

Other comments or actions:

_____

_____

_____

Additional Actions:

_____

_____

_____

Table A: World Religions by Percentage

Source Wikipedia http://en.wikipedia.org/wiki/
File:World-religions.PNG

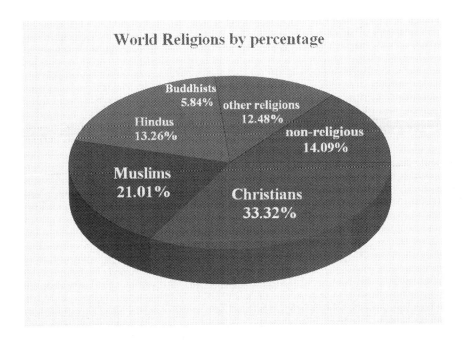

This pie chart is taken from Wikipedia, the free encyclopedia.

Source of Data: Author and Publisher: Pew Research Center. Based in Washington DC, the Pew Research Center has been a good source of data on various subjects such as patterns and relevant topics (within the country and all over the world).

url = http://pewglobal.org/reports/display.php?ReportID=167 / date = 2002-12-19}}</ref>

Table A is available under Wikipedia's Creative Commons Attribution-ShareAlike License.

Table B: Religious Groupings of the World

Religious groupings: Source Wikipedia the free Encyclopedia *http://en.wikipedia.org/wiki/Major_religious_groups*
• Abrahamic religions are the largest group, and these consist mainly of Christianity, Islam, Judaism and the Bahá'í Faith. They are named for the patriarch Abraham, and are unified by the practice of monotheism. Today, around 3.4 billion people are followers of Abrahamic religions and are spread widely around the world apart from the regions around East and Southeast Asia. Several Abrahamic organizations are vigorous proselytizers.[7]
• Indian religions originated in Greater India and tend to share a number of key concepts, such as dharma and karma. They are of the most influence across the Indian subcontinent, East Asia, Southeast Asia, as well as isolated parts of Russia. The main Indian religions are Hinduism, Jainism, Buddhism and Sikhism.
• East Asian religions consist of several East Asian religions which make use of the concept of *Tao* (in Chinese) or *Dō* (in Japanese or Korean), namely Taoism and Confucianism, both of which are asserted by some scholars to be non-religious in nature.
• African diasporic religions practiced in the Americas, imported as a result of the Atlantic slave trade of the 16th to 18th centuries, building on traditional religions of Central and West Africa.

- Indigenous <u>ethnic religions</u>, formerly found on every continent, now marginalized by the major organized faiths, but persisting as undercurrents of <u>folk religion</u>. Includes <u>traditional African religions</u>, Asian <u>Shamanism</u>, <u>Native American religions</u>, <u>Austronesian</u> and <u>Australian Aboriginal</u> traditions, <u>Chinese folk religion</u>, and postwar <u>Shinto</u>.

- <u>Iranian religions</u> (not listed below due to overlaps) originated in Iran and include <u>Zoroastrianism</u>, <u>Yazdânism</u>, <u>Ahl-e Haqq</u> and historical traditions of <u>Gnosticism</u> (<u>Mandaeism</u>, <u>Manichaeism</u>). It has significant overlaps with Abrahamic traditions, e.g. in <u>Sufism</u> and in recent movements such as <u>Bábism</u>and the <u>Bahá'í Faith</u>.

This table is taken from Wikipedia, the free encyclopedia.

Source of Data: Author and Publisher: Pew Research Center

url=http://pewglobal.org/reports/display.php?ReportID=167 / date = 2002-12-19}}</ref>

Table B is available under Wikipedia's Creative Commons Attribution-ShareAlike License.

Table C: Spoken World Languages

Language	Native speakers (in millions) [1]	% of world population	Mainly spoken in
Mandarin	935 (955)	14.1%	China, Taiwan, Malaysia, Singapore
Spanish	387 (407)	5.85%	Hispanic America, Spain, United States, Equatorial Guinea
English	365 (359)	5.52%	Australia, Canada, Ireland, New Zealand, United Kingdom, United States, South Africa, Singapore
Hindi	295 (311)	4.46%	India
Arabic	280 (293)	4.23%	North Africa, Western Asia (Middle East)
Portuguese	204 (216)	3.08%	Angola, Brazil, Mozambique, Portugal
Bengali	202 (206)	3.05%	Bangladesh, West Bengal (*India*), Tripura (*India*), Assam (*India*)
Russian	160 (154)	2.42%	Russia, former Republics of the Soviet Union, Mongolia, Israel
Japanese	127 (126)	1.92%	Japan
Punjabi	96 (102)	1.44%	Punjab region (*Pakistan, India*)

Language	Native speakers (in millions) [1]	% of world population	Mainly spoken in
German	92 (89)	1.39%	Austria, Belgium (Eupen-Malmedy), Germany, Luxembourg, Liechtenstein, Switzerland, South Tirol (Italy)

This Table is taken from Wikipedia, the free encyclopedia

Specifically, the Source is Ethnologue: Languages of the World. This is a well known language catalog, often used as a reference. However, the reader is asked to exercise some judgment as to the accuracy of some data, not only from this source, but in this topic area in general. That is due to multiple factors, such as the confusion caused by one person being multilingual, and the different protocol used to calculate such situations, as well as other issues around movement of people across the world etc.

Table of Languages of the World is available under a Creative Commons Attribution-Noncommercial license.